Table Of Contents

Foreword

This is the book every parent who cares what their children eat should be buying. If you ever wonder why your child's lunchbox comes back from school each day full of uneaten food or why your child is absolutely ravenous when they come out of school you might want to think about what you put into their 'fuel pack' for lunch.

As a grandfather to four children I know the importance of the right food choices on health, concentration and behaviour. Don't I know this stuff from my own personal experience too? I am a busy, driven man and sometimes in this life we make the wrong decisions because we are in no position to make the right decisions. What do I mean by that? I am in hotels and conference centres around the world and the food is just laid on. Without thinking things through a little I could go for all the foods that are going to make me sleepy and lacklustre. Well, how is that going to look when I step on the stage to present to my audience? That audience may have paid £1000s to hear me speak. They don't want to listen to a sleepy, lacklustre Raymond. They want a sparkly, sprightly Raymond. Now I know exactly which foods are going to help me stay sparkly and sprightly, and by the way keep me looking good too, so that I can give the audience what they expect. In fact, I can exceed their expectations and blow them away.

I want my grandchildren to have this advantage too. Imagine how much better at school they will be doing if they can stay on the ball all day, if they feel healthy, vibrant and don't have to take days off sick, thereby missing out on important learning opportunities. I want them to know that food can be fun. It doesn't have to be the same old sandwich and yogurt everyday. It can be interesting and varied with loads of choice available to them and not the choices that supermarkets want them to make. We know what supermarkets can be like, promoting the less than healthy products which reap more than healthy profits for them and less healthy rewards for our children.

So, if you want to have an edge, to be ahead of the game and to ensure your child is having a healthy lunchbox everyday, you should read this book. What's so great about it is that Jenny Tschiesche, who is a renowned nutrition expert and mother of two school-age children, has done the thinking and planning for you. She has made that daily chore of coming up with new and fresh ideas, then making them into a lunchbox that your child is going to eat a lot simpler and much less of a chore. In fact with all these new ideas you will be inspired and start enjoying the process. You may even find yourself trying these ideas yourself.

So I'd like you to raise your child's lunchbox and toast the next, healthier, generation.

Raymond Aaron
New York Times Bestselling Author
www.UltimateAuthorBootcamp.com

Acknowledgements

This book would not have been possible without the help of some highly skilled people. I would like to thank, in no particular order, the following people. Rebecca Dandy who is my proof-reader extraordinaire. Judy Hicks who edited the book. Catherine Hamm who designed the stunning covers and Werner Tschiesche who has provided more than a little support in the writing of this book.

Chapter 1: What's Wrong With Sandwiches?

As a nation, the nation that invented the sandwich, we have come to rely on this little package of two slices of bread. It is usually wrapped around some butter or margarine, filled with some type of processed meat or a large helping of mayonnaise with an added extra like tuna or egg. This has become the mainstay of any lunch eaten outside the home.

While a sandwich is a practical and easy-to-make option, it restricts the variety our children can eat. These days, with the various nut and egg free policies in schools as well as children's increasingly picky eating habits, it means they quite often end up having the same sandwich every school day. This sandwich is usually a ham or a cheese sandwich and is likely to be with white bread. The lack of fibre combined with a high salt and fat content and low levels of nutrients like vitamins and minerals make this a missed opportunity to fuel the minds and bodies of our next generation.

Although we may have the best intentions of feeding our children healthy foods, it is important to recognise that there are many factors that make it much more difficult to stick to our guns. Time pressure, finances, peer pressure, what supermarkets are selling and marketing to us, what they are allowed to eat in school and what they will actually eat can all combine against us to stop us serving our children what we would really like them to eat. Starting out being creative and resourceful with ideas for what should go into our child's lunchbox can be an exciting prospect for about the first week of the term, then it soon becomes a chore.

It's time to face the music and find out what we, as parents, can do to help improve the choices we make for our children. After all, as a London-based doctor named Dr. Harry Clements once famously said, 'Children's diseases are really parent's mistakes'.

It's a serious statement. As a parent it certainly makes me feel doubly responsible to feed my own children well. However this book is not about my children. It's about using my knowledge as a nutrition expert to help other parents and I do this from a position of empathy.

I believe the pressure on a parent to make the right food choices has never been harder. Why? Well, we'll take a look. We'll discover how to use this pressure to our advantage. We will also find ways to make much healthier and enjoyable food choices for our children with a view to improving their longer-term health.

You may think there's too much choice. But is there? When we stop and think for a moment about our choices, we might become overwhelmed believing that we have too many different foods to choose from. The adverts for small pots of yogurt filled with calcium and vitamin D, the cheese strings, triangles and shapes sell us an image of infinite choice. Are these really the choices we want to be making though?

As one of the UK's leading nutrition experts with a personal interest in the food that goes into our children's lunchboxes, I am horrified by the lack of variety in the average lunchbox. 3.6 million children in the UK, between the ages of 4-15, take a lunchbox to school every day (Mintel). That's 3.6 million lunchboxes. Recently I ran a project in which the nursery school took pictures of the contents of all the children's lunchboxes for one week. This showed that lunchboxes contained:

- A plastic pot or shaped (i.e. the shape of a fruit) yogurt, filled with sugar and very little (if any) fruit.
- A piece of reformed cheese or ham either alone or inside/alongside white bread or crackers made with white flour.
- A few cherry tomatoes or carrot sticks, although most lunchboxes had no vegetable portions.
- One piece of fruit, although most lunchboxes had none.

The market for packed lunchboxes is changing. There is much more demand for different kinds of bread, such as waffles, flatbreads, wraps and pitta pockets. We also know that there are trends for different types of protein, for instance cheese strings cheese portions and dippers. Do these latest products make our choices any easier? Does it enforce our desire to make sure our children are having a healthy balanced lunchbox? Of course not. If anything it makes our job harder because there's just more of the same - more bread without fibre, more cheese with high salt content and more peer pressure or pester power so it actually becomes harder and harder to navigate your children to the right food choices. It also makes it harder for the 'wanting to please conscience' that wants to allow your children the same foods as their friends so they don't get teased.

How well are we doing on meeting the needs of our children's 'five-a-day'?

In spite of all of the campaigns in the media and in schools to ensure all of us are eating five-a-day vegetable and fruit portions, statistically we are not doing too well in this area. A study by the School Food Trust has revealed that over 40% of lunchboxes don't contain a single piece of vegetable or fruit that could count towards the children's five-a-day.

Why are these statistics so poor?

Many of the parents I work with claim that 'it's all right because, although my child won't eat any vegetables, he/she eats fruit all the time'. No, actually that's not all right. Think about the sugar load if s/he is eating fruit sugar all day long. There are also certain nutrients, which are far more abundant in vegetables than fruit. Think about dark green vegetables and brightly coloured root vegetables. The B Vitamins and iron from the green vegetables and the beta-carotene from the root vegetables would be hard to replicate in fruit portions. There's a reason it is five-a-day vegetables and fruit and not just five-a-day fruit portions. The point is - it's important to eat vegetables.

So what constitutes a portion anyway?

Well, according to various government sources (after all they are the people who came up with the five-a day concept) these are all one portion:

Fruit	Vegetable
1 medium apple, pear	2 broccoli florets
1 handful of grapes	3 heaped tablespoons of peas
1 medium glass of fruit juice	1 cereal bowl of salad
7 strawberries	8 cauliflower florets
3 whole dried apricots	5cm piece of cucumber
1 medium banana	4 heaped tablespoons of green beans

Figure 1.1:
Vegetable and fruit portions as part of your five-a-day.

There's some work to be done in this area. Don't worry though that is what this book is for. Someone has done the thinking for you. I make it my business to know these things, and I am going to tell you just how it needs to be. Not just why but how.

What about the food choices we make and the effects on our children's health?

Well it's not a great outlook here either. There are many more behavioural problems, health conditions and allergies increasingly being linked to diet now. Children come into my clinic with all sorts of health related conditions and my first response is always to congratulate the parent for realising that food may be able to help their child. I've worked with children about to be excluded from school for behavioural issues, with children who are unable to sleep at night, children who are really picky or fussy eaters, children with multiple food allergies whose parents are worried about the diversity of their dietary choices. Let me tell you about Zac.

Case study – Zac age six.

Zac is six and had been at school for a just over a year. According to his school Zac was 'unteachable'. He was not allowed in the mainstream classes because his behaviour was so poor. Zac's Mum is amazing. She took Zac to all sorts of professionals to get him checked out yet no one could spot what the problem was and Zac was being labelled as a naughty boy. Having read one of my articles on the link between sugar intake and behavior, Zac's Mum started to reduce the amount of sugar in Zac's diet. She saw an immediate improvement in his behaviour. Once she had seen this improvement she told other people. It was then that she brought Zac to see me in person. Once we had carried out a few tests and identified problem foods we started to see real improvements in his health. Well done Zac's Mum for making the connection and doing something about it. Zac is now back in mainstream school and loving it. He loves his new diet too. I don't think either his Mum or Zac had realised just how much real choice there was, even when removing certain food groups.

Many parents simply don't make the connection. A friend of mine is a teacher and suffers from eczema, but she keeps it at bay by using the right dietary choices. She told me about a pupil in her class. This girl was also an eczema sufferer, and unsurprisingly had the worst combination of foods in her lunchbox. She is severely overweight and is eating sugar, saturated fats and salt every day for her lunch. All these foods are probably contributing to her skin condition. The teacher claims she sits scratching all day, looking really uncomfortable. If only her mum or dad knew what they could be doing to help.

Food allergies are on the rise.

Food allergy is where a child has a potentially life-threatening reaction to a food. Food intolerance is where a reaction to a food causes symptoms as varied as digestive disturbances, through headaches to skin problems.

Almost one in twelve young children now suffer from a food allergy. This number has risen dramatically in the past 40 years and continues to rise.

When I was at school, I was aware that one girl in the whole school (which had over 1000 pupils) suffered with a peanut allergy. Sadly I was to learn years later that she had died while at University from exposure to peanuts. I wonder if this is because we knew less then than we do now about these allergies. Were we ignorant about just how serious they can be? These days it is not uncommon to find a child in most classrooms with an allergy to peanuts, tree nuts, egg and/or milk, although other food allergies also exist in smaller numbers.

Food intolerance is also an issue. For some parents it is evident very early on in a child's life that eating or drinking a particular food substance can cause the child to feel ill, to experience digestive disturbances and so on, to the extent that they naturally eliminate the food or food group from their child's diet. With this in mind, the options available to parents who wish to choose a diverse lunchbox for their children may seem limited. However, this book will show you how to incorporate a wide variety of foods and cover all the nutrient groups in the 'Lunchbox checklist' (outlined in Chapter 2).

If a school has a 'no nuts policy' or if children are asked not to bring in products with egg or sesame seeds, then some of the more obvious healthy and protein boosting components of a lunchbox are automatically eliminated. This book takes that in to consideration too.

If any of these issues are a concern for you or your child then I urge you to read Chapter 8 on Food Allergy and Food Intolerance, in detail.

Parents these days have very little time.

We are all pressed for time. We live in a culture of immediacy, of instant gratification. Things need to be done and they need to be done now. As a parent, this may mean a list as long as your arm - sports kits that need washing and ironing, beds that need changing, homework that needs doing and of course packed lunchboxes that need making. Do you really have the time to sit down each week and plan your child's lunchboxes, making sure that every single day you are providing a balanced meal containing all the right nutrients for a healthy child full of vitality? Well if you don't I have some good news, and if you do I have some good news too. If you don't have time then you will find some great menu plans ready for you in Chapter 3 of this book. These are just sample menu plans but for a plan for each day of the year you can now subscribe to **www.lunchboxdoctor.com**.

Chapter 3 also provides tips and information on how to plan your weekly lunchbox menu.

Budgets are at breaking point.

It is no secret that many of us have less available income than we did five years ago. One parent may have given up work to look after the children, which means that the household's income is halved. Children, let's face it, are expensive. If it is not new shoes or clothes, it's a new computer or the latest bike. All of this means less available income to spend on food. It means that the food choices we make need to be wise ones. It's obviously easier to make suitable and financially better decisions with the right information. That's my job. Read on…

Why read this book?

The reason for writing this book is that I genuinely believe parents want to give their children the best, most balanced, healthiest lunchbox contents available. The choices available to us are not easy to make. We have too many products on the supermarket shelves that aren't suitable for children, but that are targeted and marketed at them.

I have written this book to make sure that parents have a resource that will enable them to make the right choices. This means the simplest, the healthiest, the cheapest and the quickest choices. We will also consider issues such as food allergies, food intolerances, behaviour and concentration, immune health, budget constraints, peer pressure and time constraints.

Let me take you through the five ways in which you are going to improve your child's lunchbox. By the end of this book you will be able to make fun and interesting lunchbox plans, using foods that your children will eat. Rest assured that the food choices are exactly the sort of food you should be feeding them to ensure they have the optimum fuel, not only for their day or week ahead, but for living a long and fruitful and ultimately healthy life.

This book will enable you to create a healthy balanced meal in a lunchbox, achieve two of your child's five-a-day as well as making sure that the nutritional value of what you put into your child's lunchbox is sufficient to give them plenty of energy to last the whole day.

Chapter 2: The Lunchbox Checklist

In your mind you should be able to go through a mental checklist to ensure that your child's lunchbox contains all the elements that make it a COMPLETE and BALANCED lunchbox by the end of this chapter.

There are six components to the COMPLETE and BALANCED lunchbox:

1. Carbohydrates
2. Protein
3. Calcium
4. Fruit
5. Vegetables
6. Water

Let's go through these one by one.

Carbohydrates – what are they and why do our children need them?

Carbohydrates are the body's most important and readily available source of energy. As a society we have become a little 'carb-phobic' but they are and always will be a necessary part of a healthy and balanced diet of children and adults alike.

The two major forms of carbohydrates are:

1. Simple carbohydrates – i.e. fructose, glucose, sucrose and lactose found in some healthier foods like fruits, vegetables, and dairy products but also in some less than healthy foods like donuts, cakes, biscuits, ice-cream, milkshakes.

2. Starches or complex carbohydrates which are found in foods such as starchy vegetables, grains, rice, breads and cereals.

The carbohydrates in some foods (mostly those that contain simple sugars and highly refined grains, such as white flour and white rice) are easily broken down and cause blood sugar levels to rise quickly. Sadly 'what goes up, must come down' so your child will end up with an energy high followed by an energy low if you pack their lunch with the wrong kinds of carbs. Furthermore eating a diet that's high in simple carbohydrates, which cause a rapid rise in blood sugar, will increase the risk of developing health problems like diabetes and heart disease, although these studies have been done mostly on adults.

Complex carbohydrates (found in whole grains), on the other hand, are broken down more slowly, allowing blood sugar to rise and fall more gradually.

Despite the recent craze to cut carbohydrates, the bottom line is that not all foods containing carbohydrates are bad for children, whether they're complex (as in whole grains) or simple (such as those found in fruits). If carbohydrates were really a bad thing, we'd have a huge problem on our hands as most foods contain them. Still, some carbohydrate-dense foods are healthier than others.

Healthy sources of carbohydrates include:

- whole grain cereals
- brown rice
- whole grain breads
- fruits
- vegetables
- naturally lower-fat dairy products

 For children over two-years-old, a healthy balanced diet should include 50% to 60% of calories from carbohydrates. The key is to make sure that the majority of these carbohydrates come from good sources and that any added sugar in their diet is limited.

What's so good about whole grains?

Whole grains contain all three parts of the grain (the bran, germ, and endosperm, whereas refined grains are mainly just the endosperm) and the whole means more for your body to break down. More to break down means the breakdown is slower, the carbohydrates enter the body more slowly, and it's easier for your body to regulate them.

Whole grains are high in fibre. We often associate a need for fibre with the elderly but foods that are good sources of fibre are beneficial because they're filling and therefore discourage overeating. Diets rich in whole grains protect against diabetes and heart disease. Plus, when combined with adequate fluid, they help move food through the digestive system to prevent constipation. Whole grains also contain vital vitamins and minerals including B vitamins, magnesium and iron.

Portion sizes of carbohydrates.

The actual amount of carbohydrates will vary depending on a child's age, gender and level of physical activity. However, I would suggest that between four to six portions of whole grains be eaten a day. A portion might be:

- one slice of bread;
- a small bowl of cereal;
- a half cup of cooked brown rice or cooked whole wheat pasta.

What about sugar?

The key to keeping sugar consumption in check is moderation. Added sugar can enhance the taste of some foods and a little sugar, particularly if it's in a food that provides other important nutrients such as cereal or yogurt, isn't going to tip the scales or send your child to the dentist.

 Instead of serving foods that are low in nutrients and high in added sugar, offer healthier choices such as fruit, which is a naturally sweet snack that contains carbohydrate, fibre and vitamins.

A scary statistic is that each can of fizzy drink contains on average the equivalent of TEN teaspoons of sugar and 150 calories. Instead of fizzy drinks or even juice drinks (which often contain as much added sugar as soft drinks), serve milk (or milk alternatives), water or 100% fruit or vegetable juice.

Although there's no added sugar in 100% fruit juice, the calories from the natural sugars found in fruit juice can add up. Furthermore only one glass of juice a day will count towards your child's 'five-a-day'. Adding more to their diet doesn't add more nutritional value but will add to their sugar consumption.

The best way of explaining the difference between better and poorer carbohydrate choices is by using an analogy: the hare and the tortoise.

So, this is what you tell your child. The hare eats a white bread sandwich for lunch with some strawberry jam filling. The tortoise eats a wholemeal bread sandwich with some egg and lettuce for his lunch. The hare has so much energy that he goes racing off but he soon gets tired, slows down and eventually falls asleep under the nearest tree.

The tortoise has the perfect amount of energy. Off he goes, at a gentle pace but the difference is that he can keep going on and on and on. So soon he passes the sleepy hare, who is lying there exhausted and unable to move. The tortoise is the winner because he has kept the same amount of energy all afternoon. Tell your child to imagine this at school and if they eat the lunch with the wholemeal bread they are much more likely to still have energy at the end of the day than if they eat the white bread jam sandwich.

Protein – what is it and why do our children need it?

With carbs receiving all the bad press lately, protein seems to be getting all the positive attention. It is basking in the limelight. Of course it is important to have enough protein in your complete and balanced lunchbox but it is not the be all and end all. However, sufficient amounts will help build, maintain and repair the tissues of your child's body, and help them to make sufficient antibodies (the part of the immune system that fights off infection) and haemoglobin (the part of the red blood cells that carries oxygen from the lungs to the rest of the body). Protein also helps muscle growth and improves strength. BUT eating too much protein can make the body lose calcium, which is necessary to build strong bones.

Protein is made up of amino acids. There are a total of 20 amino acids, but our bodies only produce 14, so we have to get the other six from food. Protein is found in milk, meat, eggs, nuts, seeds, pulses, legumes, poultry, fish and shellfish.

 Don't worry if your child is a vegetarian because they too can get sufficient amounts of protein by eating combinations of legumes and grains like soy and rice.

How much protein does my child need?

The recommended daily intake of protein depends on body weight. Ideally 0.5 grams(g) of protein for every pound(lb) of body weight. For example a child who weighs 50lbs (about three and a half stone) should have about 25g of protein every day.

The best way to explain protein to your child.

Protein foods are those foods that your child needs in order to grow and in order to repair cuts and wounds.

Calcium – what is it and why do our children need it?

We all associate the mineral calcium with strong bones. Building strong bones predominantly happens towards the earlier years of our children's lives. By the time they get to the end of their teenage years they will either have strong bones or they won't - so ensuring that they get sufficient calcium (as well as other supporting nutrients) when they are young is critical. Bone calcium begins to decrease in young adulthood and progressive loss of bone occurs as we age, particularly in women.

Teenagers, especially girls, whose diets don't provide the nutrients to build bones to their maximum potential are at greater risk of developing the bone disease osteoporosis, which increases the risk of fractures.

Younger children and babies with little calcium and vitamin D intake (vitamin D helps calcium absorption) are at increased risk for rickets. Rickets is a bone-softening disease that causes severe bowing of the legs, poor growth and sometimes muscle pain and weakness.

Calcium also plays important roles in muscle contraction, transmitting messages through the nerves, and the release of hormones. If blood calcium levels are low (due to poor calcium intake), calcium is taken from the bones to ensure normal cell function. This will obviously affect the strength of the bones.

Children need to consume sufficient amounts of calcium and vitamin D but they also need sufficient weight-bearing exercise to keep their bones healthy. When children get enough calcium, vitamin D and physical activity during childhood and the teen years, they can start out their adult lives with the strongest bones possible, which will be beneficial to them for their entire lives.

How much calcium does my child need?

The British Dietetic Association has created a useful system for parents to work out what these amounts actually look like. If 50mg calcium is 1 point then these food portions provide various points.

- A child 6-12 months needs 5.4 points of calcium a day (see chart below).
- A child 1-3 years needs 10 points of calcium a day
- A child 4-8 years needs 16 points of calcium a day
- A child 9-18 years needs 26 points of calcium a day

Calcium Points	Portion Size
5	1 pot (150g) plain yogurt, ⅓ pint milk ½ tin sardines in tomato sauce 50g (2oz) tofu
4	30g (2oz) Cheddar cheese 30g (1oz) Edam cheese Large serving of spring greens/ okra / kale / spinach, boiled (130g or 5oz) ⅓ pint calcium enriched soya or rice milk
3	1 tbsp Parmesan cheese 1 medium cheese scone ½ small tin pilchards in tomatosauce 3 dried figs 125 ml (small pot) of calcium-enriched soya yoghurt 2 wholemeal bread
2	1 pot (100g) fromage frais ½ small tin canned salmon small tub cottage cheese small bar milk chocolate (i.e. small Green and Blacks) ½ large tin kidney beans
1	⅓ pint soya milk 1 small tin baked beans 9 brazil nuts (30g) 8 dried non-sulphured apricot halves

Figure 2.1:
Calcium portion sizes.

Getting enough calcium is just part of the equation. We are suffering from a national Vitamin D deficiency problem and children are no different. Vitamin D improves the absorption of calcium into the blood stream.

The best food sources of vitamin D are:

- oily fish such as sardines, salmon and mackerel;
- eggs;
- fortified cereals.

The best way to explain calcium to your child.

Calcium is the single most important nutrient for strong bones. So think about something that is important to your child that requires strong bones, maybe dancing or sport, and describe how eating sufficient calcium will allow them to practice for longer and be a better dancer or sportsperson.

Vegetables and fruit.

They have been listed in this order deliberately. Although a lot of children enjoy fruit, fewer enjoy their vegetables. This is a problem. While both vegetables and fruit provide vitamins, minerals and dietary fibre, fruit is far higher in sugar, which is a simple carbohydrate. Vegetables contain far less sugar generally and are able to provide as much nutritional value, if not more. When the government set out their five-a-day policy they didn't expect people to aim for just five fruits per day and no vegetables and yet this is often the case. Parents are prompting their children to eat lots of fruit in order to replace the lack of vegetables, which some children appear reluctant to eat. They may be reluctant, but all is not lost. See Chapter 4 for great ways to include vegetables in your children's diet, sometimes without them even knowing.

Water and other drinks.

Water makes up a significant percentage of our body weight and we cannot survive for more than a few days without it. Blood contains a lot of water. Our blood is responsible for carrying oxygen to all the cells of our body. Without oxygen, those tiny cells would die and our bodies would stop working.

Water is also in lymph, a fluid that is part of our immune system, which helps us fight off illness.

We all need water to be able to digest food and to get rid of waste too. Water is needed for digestive juices, wee, poo and is also present in our sweat.

Our body doesn't only get water from drinking water. Lots of foods contain water too. Fruit contains quite a bit of water, which you probably have noticed if you've ever bitten into a slice of melon or mango and felt the juices dripping down your chin. Vegetables contain a lot of water too — think of slicing into plump cucumber from the garden or crunching into a crisp stalk of celery.

How much water is enough?

There is no amount that suits all, but regular intake throughout the day is best. More is needed when it's warm outside, when you have a cold/flu and are losing fluids through sweating, coughing and sneezing or when you're exercising.

When you drink is also important. Drink regularly otherwise you will find all sorts of things won't work.

We know that if we don't drink enough, we are unable to concentrate as well which could be a problem if there is an assignment at school. Also if there's insufficient fluid in our bodies we certainly cannot perform as well physically, so dance or sport's performance will be affected too.

When our body doesn't have enough water it becomes dehydrated. Dehydration will stop your child from being as fast and as sharp as he/she would like to be. In serious cases, dehydration can make you sick. So keep that water bottle handy when the weather warms up. Not only does water fight dehydration, it's wonderfully refreshing and has no calories.

How to explain the need for water to your children.

Get a large sheet of paper. Ask your child to lie down. If you have another child, get them to draw around the first child using a marker pen. Then get them both to colour in 70% of the body in blue. This then shows them how much of their body is made up of water. Then they can really see why it is so important to replace what is lost through breathing, sweat and going to the toilet.

Chapter 3: Improvement One – Planning Your Menus

The single action of planning your weekly lunchbox menus will give you peace of mind, reduce the amount you spend on lunchbox items and reduce the amount of food that you throw out each week. In short, it is time well spent.

The advantages include:

1. Providing a nutritional balance in your child's lunchbox by ensuring that the all components of Chapter 2's checklist are included.

2. Control on food budget. Some food items, such as sun-dried tomatoes and some cold meats, are so highly priced these days that they may be included as luxuries, perhaps once a week. The rest of the week's menu could be built on less expensive staples such as beans, pulses, pasta, vegetables and fruit. It is a lot easier to see what you are spending when it is laid out on a weekly plan.

3. Saving fuel. You will need to make fewer trips to the shops because you will buy what you need in one or two visits every week.

4. Saving electricity or gas. You can double up when cooking certain foods like baking two things in the oven at once.

5. More variety. When you look at the week's plan you will be able to see if they include the same or similar lunches everyday. As adults we don't like having the same food every single day and

it is not good for us nutritionally. The same applies to our children.

6. Using up leftovers. Using up cooked rice, potatoes and pasta the following day or adding leftover vegetables to a salad can be a really useful way of making the most of leftovers and creates far less waste.

7. Providing for personal likes and dislikes. Using this method of planning you can cater for your children's likes and dislikes. Adults have unique preferences and tastes and our children do as well. As one of seven siblings, I know this only too well - I am still not entirely sure how my parents coped. However, with two children of my own and with very different tastes, it means some careful thought and planning goes a long way.

Think about a few quick and easy swaps from less healthy lunchbox components to healthier lunchbox components.

Instead of:	Consider:
Higher-fat lunch meats, such as ham or salami	Lower-fat lunch meats, such as turkey or chicken, smoked salmon
White bread	Whole grain breads (wheat, oat, multi-grain)
Sandwiches	Savoury flapjacks and muffins, rice and pasta salads
Mayonnaise	Light mayonnaise, mustard, natural yogurt or fromage frais, cream cheese
Fried crisps and snacks	Baked crisps, bagel chips, popcorn, seeds, vegetable batons and dip
Fruit in syrup	Fruit in natural juices or fresh fruit
Biscuits, cakes and cereal bars	Trail mix, yogurt, granola, or homemade baked goods such as oat biscuits, flapjacks or fruit muffins
Fruit drinks or fizzy drinks	Water, milk, non-dairy milk-alternatives, fruit juice (100% fruit)

Figure 3.1:
Simple swap from less healthy to more healthy lunchbox contents.

The ideal way to plan your menu for the week is to sit down with a pen and paper, or your spreadsheet depending on what kind of planner you are, and think about:

1. What you will be having for your main meals each evening – this tells you whether you are likely to have any suitable leftovers. Things such as a soup, stew, risotto rice or cooked pasta can all be made into something suitable for a lunchbox. Alternatively you may be left with some of the raw ingredients such as cheese or some carrots.

2. What you already have in the kitchen cupboards, fridge and freezer that may be suitable for lunchboxes. For example:

    a. You might have some frozen cooked prawns or frozen mixed vegetables - both could be added to rice to make a rice salad. Prawns can be served with a dipping sauce.

    b. You may have some big packets of tortilla chips or some bagels that need using up that you can bake into bagel chips with a little garlic oil.

    c. You may even have some flour, eggs and vegetables or fruit that need using up. Muffins, either sweet (fruit) or savoury (vegetable) are a great way of using up other foods. The muffin recipes are available in Chapter 9 of this book.

3. What foods your child enjoys most, and which ones they enjoy least.

4. What foods or food groups your child is not trying. You can refer to the end of Chapter 4 for the section on Fussy Eating to find ways of incorporating these foods into their lunchbox.

5. How to include all the items on the complete and balanced lunchbox checklist in Chapter 2.

A note on making the most of your freezer

If you know how to use your freezer properly you can open up a whole world of opportunities as far as packed lunch planning is concerned.

What can you freeze?

Most importantly you should be familiar with what can and what cannot be frozen. For example did you know that you can freeze dairy products like milk and cheese? You can also freeze meat (cooked or not), pastry, cakes, vegetables and bread.

Freezing bread in portion sizes: The concept of freezing bread in portion sizes that are suitable for your family's usage is such a time and money saver. Freeze in two or four slice portions in individual freezer bags.

Vegetables - If you're really organised you could even buy a big batch of your families favourite vegetable when it's in season (and therefore at its cheapest) and freeze to use a bit at a time over the next few months.

Defrosting - These are the golden rules to abide by:

1. Never refreeze something that's already been frozen. Packaging should state if it has already been frozen. Fish has often already been frozen for example.

2. Always check the packaging. Don't freeze anything that doesn't state it's suitable for home freezing.

3. Defrost properly. Whatever you're defrosting, get it out of the freezer the night before you need it and ensure it's defrosted properly before you eat it. You can also defrost in the microwave. If you're reheating something after it has been frozen, make sure you cook it until it's piping hot throughout.

Storing in the freezer

Close up the bag, box or wrap the food tightly in cling film or suitable wrapping before freezing. This prevents freezer burn, which will spoil the taste of your food. The less air is around the product when you wrap it, the better.

Making a plan.

Once you have read the chapters of this book that are most pertinent to you, you can create a planning grid per child, (unless you are lucky and all your children eat the same things, in which case just use one grid). You can then fill in the items that match the checklist for each day of the week.

On the next page are some sample plans for you to look at to give you some ideas on how to put these planning hints and tips into action. You can have more than one item for each of the categories on the checklist. For example you might have both cheese and yogurt on a particular day, which are both sources of calcium. Equally, as is the case with the vegetable muffin, you can have more than one category mixed in one food item. For example the vegetable muffins include both carbohydrates and vegetables.

Sample Lunchbox - Week One

WEEKLY MENU PLAN

	CARBOHYDRATE	PROTEIN	CALCIUM	FRUIT	VEGETABLE	DRINK
MONDAY						
Vegetable muffin* with sliced cheese or individually wrapped cheeses	✓	✓	✓		✓	
Cherry tomatoes				✓		
Natural yogurt with honey		✓	✓			
Bottle of water						✓
TUESDAY						
Left-over cooked rice with peas, sweet corn and chopped sausage	✓	✓			✓	
Celery sticks filled with low fat cream cheese		✓	✓		✓	
Pear				✓		
Carton of milk		✓	✓			✓
WEDNESDAY						
Couscous with roasted vegetables and spoonful cream cheese	✓	✓	✓		✓	
Hard boiled egg		✓				
A mango hedgehog				✓		
Chocolate coconut milk						✓
THURSDAY						
Tuna and sweet corn (mixed with natural yogurt) sandwich on multigrain wrap	✓	✓	✓		✓	
Mini pot baked-beans (try them cold!)		✓	✓		✓	
Grapes				✓		
Natural yogurt		✓	✓			
Bottle of water						✓
FRIDAY						
Slice of vegetable quiche or pizza	✓	✓	✓		✓	
Carrot sticks					✓	
Tahini and raspberry flapjack*	✓	✓	✓	✓		
Carton of rice milk			✓			✓

Figure 3.2:
Sample lunchbox contents week 1.

* Recipes and instructions for all starred lunchbox content ideas can be found in Chapter 9

Sample Lunchbox - Week Two

WEEKLY MENU PLAN

	CARBOHYDRATE	PROTEIN	CALCIUM	FRUIT	VEGETABLE	DRINK
MONDAY						
Spinach and ricotta muffin*	✓	✓	✓		✓	
Natural yogurt with apple fruit puree			✓	✓		
Mango hedgehog				✓		
Bottle of water						✓
TUESDAY						
Baby croc guac* with carrot stick, and sugar snap dippers					✓	
Left-over cooked rice with peas and sweet corn	✓				✓	
Apple				✓		
Two squares dark chocolate	✓					
Carton of milk		✓	✓			✓
WEDNESDAY						
Oatcakes and mackerel pate	✓	✓	✓			
Cucumber batons					✓	
Strawberries				✓		
Small pot granola	✓			✓		
Fruit juice with sparkling mineral water				✓		✓
THURSDAY						
Aubergine and tahini dip * and beetroot hummus with baked pitta chips	✓	✓	✓		✓	
Pear and fromage frais			✓	✓		
Two oat biscuits	✓					
Bottle of water						✓
FRIDAY						
Savoury flapjack* made with courgettes and carrots	✓	✓			✓	
Fruit salad				✓		
Natural yogurt and honey			✓			
100% fruit juice carton				✓		✓

Figure 3.3:
Sample lunchbox contents week 2.

* Recipes and instructions for all starred lunchbox content ideas can be found in Chapter 9

These are just sample menu plans. To access weekly lunchbox plans go to **www.lunchboxdoctor.com**.

This book is full of ideas of what to put in your child's lunchbox by checklist category i.e. carbohydrate, protein, calcium, vegetable, fruit and drink. This makes your job of planning your children's lunchbox contents extremely easy. In Appendix 1 you will find a template to put together your own plan on a weekly basis for your child or children. The following chapters outline areas that you may want to consider for your own child such as producing a lunchbox on a budget, or achieving two of your child's 'five-a-day'. With the information from these chapters you can then use the template to form your child's most ideal lunchbox plan.

Chapter 4: Improvement Two – Five-a-Day Made Easy

When I asked a local nursery school to take pictures of the lunchboxes that were being brought in, I was deeply shocked and concerned at how many parents seemed to be either unaware or completely ignoring the UK Government's five-a-day advice. Maybe I was being naïve but I assumed everybody knew about this campaign. I also assumed that most parents would automatically act on the information, once they were aware of the benefits.

Well the campaign is clearly not resonating with many parents and even if they are aware of it, they don't seem to recognise that the five-a-day advice is not a limit or nice-to-have option. Five portions of vegetables and fruit is an essential minimum for good health. If we choose to ignore this, we are setting ourselves up, but more importantly our children, for a lifetime of ill health and other problems.

Back to my research: I observed that the average lunchbox consisted of a ham or cheese sandwich on white bread; a yogurt that probably contained more sugar than fruit; some crisps and maybe, if they were lucky, some fruit. I saw very few vegetables of any kind. The nutrient content was so poor I felt that some parents either were victims of severe fussy eating behaviours or believed that the lunchbox for their toddlers and young children was merely a snack, and not sustenance. Furthermore I hoped that it wasn't reflective of the meals these children were having outside of the nursery school environment.

When I look around at supermarket foods, especially those targeted at parents who are responsible for filling lunchboxes on a daily basis, they are so often devoid of actual nutrition. Unfortunately they are also loaded with sugar and salt so that parents can be assured that their children will want to eat them.

Let's revisit, for a moment, the table showing what a portion of fruit or vegetables looks like, and remember that children's portion sizes will be smaller because they are smaller. If you are wondering just how much smaller, then a portion size is the same size as their hand, i.e. one handful should be just perfect for most fruits and vegetables.

Fruit or Vegetable	Portion Size Equal to 1 of '5-a-day'
Apricots, Kiwis	2 small fruits
Apple, Pear, Banana	1 medium fruit
Melon	1 slice
100% vegetable or fruit juice	150ml
Chickpeas, baked beans, lentils	3 heaped tablespoon's
Carrots, sweetcorn	3 heaped tablespoon's
Salad	1 cereal bowlful

Figure 4.1:
Portion sizes of vegetable and fruit as part of your five-a-day.

Now, allow me to show you just how easy it might be to put together a lunchbox that contains 2 or 3 of your children's five-a-day using the checklist for the COMPLETE and BALANCED lunchbox outlined in Chapter 2.

Carbohydrate choices that incorporate vegetable and fruit portions:

- Using the savoury muffin as your base recipe (see recipes in Chapter 9), vary the contents of the muffin to include different vegetables. Some children won't touch spinach in real life but will certainly eat it in a creamy little muffin combined with some ricotta cheese.

- As a sandwich filling mix grated carrot and Red Leicester cheese. Alternatively this same mixture could be served as a cheesy coleslaw.

- Add chopped dried apricots or raisins to rice and other vegetables to make a rice salad.

- A vegetable fritter made by combining polenta (corn meal) with eggs and peas or sweet corn is a sweet tasting little package that your child may enjoy, again because they cannot see any overtly vegetable like object.

Protein choices that incorporate vegetable and fruit portions:

- Hummus made with chickpeas or white beans such as butter beans or cannellini beans. Some children may enjoy the addition of carrot or beetroot juice to their hummus which makes fun colours but also makes the hummus sweeter in flavour.

- Baked beans – in single portion size, ideally the reduced salt and sugar versions.

Calcium choices that incorporate vegetable and fruit portions:

- Combine cubes of cheddar cheese with olives or pineapple chunks, grapes or sliced apple.

- Cottage cheese with pineapple and/or grapes is often liked by children.

- Natural yogurt with some tinned prunes or tinned pears/peaches/apricots (all in natural juices).

- Whizz fruit into a milkshake with fresh milk in seconds. This can be frozen then put into a lunchbox the next morning so that by lunchtime it is the perfect temperature for drinking.

Vegetable choices:

- Vegetable kebabs, raw or cooked, go down well with many children.

- Soup (served in a Thermos flask) made with sweet and starchy root vegetables and thickened with lentils, or a roasted red pepper soup that is naturally so sweet children will barely believe they are eating real vegetables.

- Try serving familiar vegetables in unfamiliar ways.
    - Fine ribbons of cucumber are sometimes more visually appealing and appetising that great big chunks or batons for example.
    - Use a crinkle cutter to chop carrots to look like crinkle cut chips then roast with olive oil until cooked evenly.

- Wrap blanched asparagus in Parma ham.
- Slice vegetables really finely using a julienne slicer or a sharp knife. Wrap in rice paper and serve with a sweet Asian style dip.

- Popcorn can be served with various sweet or savoury toppings or even as is – just plain.

- Opt for shop-bought or home-cooked vegetable chips such as beetroot, parsnip and sweet potato.

- Try mini versions of vegetables such as mini sweet corn cobs, cherry tomatoes, baby carrots or baby beetroot.

- Sugar snaps (raw) are lovely and sweet, as are pepper strips. These work really well with dips such as hummus, guacamole, cottage cheese or mackerel pate.

Fruit choices:

- Make fruit kebabs.

- Allow the children to enjoy the fun of fruits that lend themselves to fun ways of presentation such as the mango cheek, which you can slice and then score the flesh in a criss-cross pattern before turning inside out to produce a mango hedgehog.

- Use dried fruit (30g portions) alone, in baking or salads as above.

Drink choices that incorporate vegetable and fruit portions:

- 100% vegetable juices such as carrot juice, tomato juice or beetroot juice.

- Squeeze or slice lemon, lime or kiwi into your child's water bottle.

- Combine fruit juice with sparkling mineral water. This is a great fizzy drink alternative.

Explaining the importance of vegetables and fruit to your children:

As adults we know that vegetables and fruit are full of goodness. They contain a wide range of antioxidants, vitamins, minerals and other plant-based chemicals that benefit our health. These are all naturally occurring and help protect the cells in our bodies.

Vegetables and fruit are full of fibre, which helps us to digest our food effectively and efficiently. In the longer term, a good intake of fibre has been shown to help lower the level of bad fat (cholesterol) in our blood stream and also reduce the risk of bowel cancer.

To explain antioxidants to your child have them core, peel and slice an apple (if they are younger, they may need some help with this). Spread out the pieces and ask your child what you think will happen to the apple in the next 15 minutes.

Next get them to do exactly the same with a second apple but after slicing the apple dip it into a solution of vitamin C and water (made by dissolving a chewable or dissolvable vitamin C tablet in water), or using fresh lemon juice.

After 15 minutes they will notice that the apple exposed to the air is brown. This is called 'oxidation'. They will also notice that the apple in the vitamin C solution has not turned brown. The vitamin C has protected the apple. Vitamin C is what is known as an 'antioxidant'.

Oxidation is what happens every day in our bodies, more oxidation occurs if we make the wrong food choices such as eating too much fatty and fried foods and too much sugar. We need to consume enough antioxidants to make sure that too much oxidation doesn't take place. Ironically apples also contain vitamin C and are in no way bad for us but the reaction of the apple in the air is just a good way of showing what is happening inside our bodies all the time.

Some vegetables and fruit are labelled as 'superfoods' because they contain particularly high concentrations of some phytonutrients, particularly antioxidants. You may want to highlight these as 'superheroes', using your children's favourite characters as comparisons.

- Blueberries - contain flavonoids that can improve circulation and help defend against infection.

- Broccoli - rich in the antioxidants vitamin C and beta-carotene, as well as folate, all of which can protect against cardiovascular disease and cancer.

- Tomatoes - rich in lycopene, a powerful antioxidant that can protect against harmful free radicals.

Variety is the key. In addition to these phytonutrients, each variety of vegetables and fruit contains its own combination of vitamins, minerals and fibre. Choosing a variety throughout the day will provide a diverse package of essential nutrients.

How to help your fussy eater?

If your child is what you would term a 'fussy eater' they will undoubtedly be fussy when it comes to vegetables and fruit, and it's likely vegetables will be more problematic than fruit. Here are a whole host of top tips in managing your fussy eater:

1. Make the lunchbox look appealing.

If it doesn't look colourful and appetising to you, it won't look nice to them either, so they are less likely to get stuck in. Think about appealing colours in your child's lunchbox, like carrots, red pepper, apples, cucumber. Some may be ignored to start with but eventually they get eaten. Keep trying as they won't be ignored forever.

2. Make it as easy to eat as possible.

These days' children don't want to hang around at lunchtime to eat, and sometimes they don't have the option. They may only have fifteen minutes or so before they are encouraged to get outside. Make lunch as easy for them as possible. Have things in bite size portions or serve finger foods. If you are worried about hygiene of using fingers for food at lunchtime then either include a wipe or put in a mini fork or spoon. Ensure lids are easy to open and that nothing has the potential to get too messy. An example is melon. While my daughter loves melon from the skin at home, she always asks me to cut it up into cubes when she is taking it to school in her packed lunch. The difference is that at home she has a sink and kitchen roll nearby. At school she is in the school hall and having to get away to wash her face would mean less playtime.

3. Get them to help prepare their lunchbox.

As with all food preparation whether it is baking or stirring the stew for supper, children are much more likely to eat their lunch if they've had a hand in making it. Encourage them to help out with the preparation - dependant on age, of course. Make it fun. Sometimes my two will help grate the vegetables or cheese for homemade muffins, often eating the food along the way (another reminder for them of how good things like vegetables can taste, especially when raw).

4. Get them to express their preferences.

Try and use their favourites as a basis, then keep the lunchbox balanced. An example might be that your child prefers not to have sandwiches but likes small bite-size chunks of foods such as cheese and grapes or likes rice and pasta dishes. You can use the same base but vary the components.

5. Variety is key.

We all like variety, otherwise we get bored, so keep the lunchbox interesting. One of the outcomes of the lunchbox exercise that the nursery school carried out was that some children had the same lunchbox every day for a week. Even if they enjoyed the food at the start of the week, the same thing day in and day out certainly became boring and unsurprisingly the children started to turn their noses up by the end of the week. I realise that we are limited in terms of what we can put into a child's lunchbox but listing all the things your child likes and rotating them, with the additional new food, can really help them to stay interested.

6. Keep the container smelling fresh.

Do not underestimate the power of smell. A lot of schools are very warm these days all year round. Lunch containers can often start to sweat. With the increase in heat and moisture, it is ripe playing field for opportunistic bacteria. The sort of bacteria that could be harmful to your child are those that can make the lunch container start to reek of mould. This is an unappealing smell and certainly doesn't encourage the child who is sitting with it right under their nose, to eat the contents of this smelly plastic sack. To keep it fresh, wipe out each evening, and leave to air overnight.

 Put a sprig of fresh parsley in to the lunchbox to keep it neutralised.

46

7. Make sure the lunch container looks good.

These lunch containers get thrown about, shoved under seats, scratched and scrapped. Rest assured, like the expensive school shoes that you bought at the beginning of term, the lunch container will start to look tired well before you expect it to. Imagine eating off a dirty, mangled plate. The good news is that a new lunch container doesn't cost a ridiculous amount these days and new kit always adds to the excitement around the whole eating experience.

8. Preparation and planning is key.

I've said it before, I've even written a whole chapter on the subject (Chapter 3) but the planning and preparation process is time well spent in encouraging your child to eat a wide and varied diet. A little thought goes a long way.

9. Keep the food cool.

As I have mentioned, schools are hot places where bacteria can create multiple bacteria families very quickly. You must keep your child's lunch container cool using an appropriate cooling block or foods. This will also make the food much more appealing. Have you ever tried a piece of warm sweaty cheese or a warm smelly yogurt? Unappealing, isn't it? If it is unappealing to us, it is unappealing for our children too. Of course you knew that, but it is sometimes hard to imagine how warm and sweaty their food might get at school. It can seem very different from when it's been packed straight from the fridge.

This chapter has provided you with the knowledge and tools, as well as some ideas, on how to achieve at least two portions of vegetables and fruit in your child's lunch container daily. It has also given you some ideas for things to consider if you are dealing with a fussy eater, be it a phase or a longer-term issue. If you would like to put these ideas into a plan for your child's lunchbox then you can use the template provided in Appendix 1.

Chapter 5: Improvement Three - Overcoming The Pressure To 'Do The Right Thing'

In this chapter we talk about the very real concerns many parents have about the ongoing health of their children in relation to their dietary habits.

- Do you worry about your child getting a sufficiently balanced diet?

- Do the obesity statistics worry you?

- Does the number of children suffering with eating disorders and body image problems concern you?

- Do you struggle to get your child to eat vegetables?

- Is your child easily seduced by free plastic toys and other marketing materials that come with certain foods?

- Has your child started to become brand-aware and express strong preferences?

- Do you feel that your child's health may benefit from eating a broader range of foods?

- Do you believe your child could have a better relationship with food?

If you have answered 'yes' to any of the above then let me reassure you that you are not alone with these concerns. In fact, when we look at the statistics, we can see our concerns are based on real fact.

1. In England in the academic year 2010/11, 9.4% of Reception (ages 4-5 years) children were obese. In the same year 19% of Year 6 (ages 10-11 years) children were obese[1].

2. A health survey carried out in South Australia in 1995, and then repeated in 2005, showed the number of people with an eating disorder doubled to almost 1 in 20 over the course of 10 years[2].

These are just a couple of examples of the dramatic ways in which the lives and eating habits of our children, and our responsibility as parents, have changed in the past fifteen years.

As parents, we are constantly under pressure to do the right thing for our children. Whether it is ensuring that they don't watch too much TV, or that they wear age-appropriate clothing, or whether it is making sure they eat the right kinds of foods. Let's take a look at what our children are exposed to and how it influences their food choices.

Celebrity endorsements and sponsorship.

There are many links between sports, sports people and events and junk food brands. Let's look at a few examples of what we are up against. Currently:

1. Key sports icons are heading up advertising campaigns for less healthy snack foods e.g. Gary Lineker and Walkers potato crisps.

---

[1] Statistics on obesity, physical activity and diet: England, 2012. NHS
[2] http://www.disordered-eating.co.uk/

2. The 2012 London Olympics was sponsored by Coca Cola, Cadbury's and McDonalds.

In the past:

3. Cadbury's had a major marketing drive (May 2003) to get children to exchange chocolate wrappers for school sports equipment. The Labour Health Minister, Melanie Johnson worked out that children would have to eat 5,440 chocolate bars, or almost 1.25 million calories, to get a set of free volleyball posts.

4. The BBC licensed the Tweenies, a brand targeted at pre-school children, to be used by both McDonalds and Burger King. In 2001 the total Tweenies franchise earned the BBC over £32m.

Too much choice.

Think about the following - when you were growing up, do you remember there being a choice of 136 different yogurt-style desserts? Do you remember there being a whole aisle in the supermarket dedicated to such products? What about having to choose from over 60 types of crisps or potato chips, in another dedicated aisle? Weren't supermarkets in fact smaller partly because there were fewer products and less choice?

The pressure (and sometimes hysteria) of the media, governments and other parents.

We are constantly under pressure from:

1. The media – newspapers or parenting magazines saying what you should and shouldn't be feeding your children.

2. The government – reminding us all through the curriculum that we should be eating so many portions of vegetables and fruit a day.

3. The schools – some tell the children that they have 'good' food or 'bad' food in their lunchboxes.

4. The supermarkets and food manufacturers – who make claims about how 'healthy' their products are.

5. Other parents – who either directly or indirectly pass comment on the way you feed your children and how they feed theirs.

What with these and the many other pressures that we face in daily life is it any wonder that parents do not know where to turn?

Poor nutrition education.

The reality of the matter is that most children, through not fault of their own, have very little knowledge on the subject of nutrition. Home Economics and Domestic Science is not only a dying subject at schools, but even if you do take it up at school you are more likely to learn about manufacturing food than cooking it. Any domestic science for younger children will inevitably involve baking or decorating cakes and biscuits with sugary icing and sweets or candies. While it is fun teaching and learning about cake decoration, it seems that baking and cake decorating are disproportionately represented as far as cooking skills are concerned.

Food companies that target children.

Junk food companies entice children to the high fat and high sugar options (to which we are naturally disposed due to our cave-man like instincts to fuel up quickly when we can) by presenting lovely free gifts such as plastic characters from their favourite films. Unfortunately children are predisposed to want colourful plastic toys and therefore the high-fat meal, the bag of crisps or the chocolate dessert that comes with it. Of course most parents realise they are being duped, but the persuasive powers of our children are strong and if the parents are feeling tired or worn out, they get stronger. Once a few parents have given in to the persuasion of their children whining and moaning, others do too and then everyone is on a slippery slope because nobody wants their children feeling different or excluded. They too buy the 'foods with benefits' for their children.

It is difficult to know where to go for information and who to trust. However, against this backdrop of pressure, we can fight back with some tricks of our own, thanks to this book.

Top tips for using 'peer' pressure and TV/media to our advantage:

1. Give new names to old foods – whether it is home-made green smoothies called 'Shrek-Juice' or 'Baby Croc Guac' (See recipes in Chapter 9) for guacamole, children find quirky and fun names make the foods much more appealing.

2. Use stickers or labels on foods to make them just as appealing if not more so than some of the manufacturers fancy packaging. An experiment carried out on children in the US found that they found the taste of carrot sticks served in the same packaging as one of their favourite crisps brands more appealing and sweeter tasting than those served simply on their own. The important message here is that the wrapping of foods can be as important as the content of the food itself. Of course you can invest in expensive food wrappings and you can even buy stickers from various sites on the Internet, but why not get your children to design their own stickers or packaging.

3. Present foods in a way that makes your child's lunchbox interesting to their friends. My daughter's friend thinks her 'mango hedgehog' is genius. She has told the whole class about how clever it is. It's not really, but it certainly makes the children want to eat it. How much nicer is it to have a homemade piece of cake or flapjack every now and then? Homemade carrot cake tastes so much better and it's certain that all your children's friends would merrily ditch

their shop-bought plastic for some of the deep, dark, rich and sticky alternative.

4. Get the children involved in a little maths by calculating the number of portions of vegetables and fruit in their lunchbox each day and adding it to a chart.

5. Find a TV character, sports star or personality that your children like and either find evidence of a positive and healthy behaviour or make one up (depending on the character and age of the child) to emphasize the importance of eating the right kinds of foods most often. For example, Andy Murray's favourite food is sushi, but equally you could tell your youngster that their favourite cartoon character eats courgettes. Remember Popeye?

6. Try not to be too influenced by the ever-changing 'fads' you read about in the newspapers regarding what you should and shouldn't be feeding your children. Use this book and the website **www.lunchboxdoctor.com** as your trusted resource for information on children's complete and balanced lunchboxes. If the answer isn't obvious then go to the 'contact me' page and ask me.

7. Find the brands that you trust but do check the labels from time to time because they do change the ingredients or methods used in making the product occasionally.

8. If you are introducing new foods to your child make sure you try them out at home or with friends first. It may be that you choose to have a

picnic tea involving some newer foods. You may decide to invite some of your child's friends round for a special tea after school and introduce the new foods that way. They are less likely to be completely rejected if they have at least seen the new foods before.

9. Get your children involved in cookery classes or get them involved in cooking at home – or both. There are a whole host of opportunities up and down the country to get children as young as two involved in cooking. There is also a great blog by Nick Coffer called www.mydaddycooks.com offering recipes that you can try with your child.

10. Many schools get the children involved in projects such as designing a healthy lunchbox or healthy eating. On the **www.lunchboxdoctor.com** website you will find some sample menu plans that your child's school can use for such projects. By using these in their projects, and perhaps even making some of the recipes, your children will be introduced to some foods which will become more sociably acceptable because their peers will have seen them and been exposed to them too.

Here are some ideas for presenting food in a way, using this pressure to your advantage by looking at the checklist items from Chapter 2:

Carbohydrate choices that support parental pressures:

- Make oatcakes but use a cookie cutter in the shape of your child's favourite TV character, or a snowman if it is winter, or a Christmas tree if it Christmas and so on.

- Individual bread rolls give a personal touch so either shop bought or homemade can work better than sliced bread sometimes.

- Stick to plain flavoured or baked crisps to reduce the chance of sweeteners, flavours, preservatives and high levels of salt and saturated fat BUT allow your child to choose. You can now buy baked crisps, root vegetable crisps, rice cakes, bagel chips, tortillas and baked pitta chips. All, generally healthier choices than the majority of the other crisps and all in the same supermarket aisle. Serve either in the bags they come in, or buy a big bag and decant into smaller bags.

Protein choices that support parental pressures:

- Rather than buy expensive, individually wrapped cheese slices or cheese strings, chop your own block of cheese into little chunks and serve wrapped in homemade or designed greaseproof paper or in a small pot.

- Rather than buy processed meats, allow your child to see you slice meat fresh from the Sunday roast leftovers.

- Compartmentalised lunchboxes or pots allow you to serve lots of smaller portions of dips for example or a variety of foods such as cold baked beans and some mini sausages. This means your child is unlikely to be overwhelmed by a large portion of one food that they may not particularly enjoy.

Calcium choices that support parental pressures:

- Where yogurt is concerned, there is simply too much choice and most of it's unhealthy. I would opt for good old natural yogurt and allow your child the choice of any one of the many fruit purees, tinned fruit, dried fruit, trail mixes, granola, cereal or honey as a topping. You see how much choice there is and the choice can be your child's own, every single day of the week.

- Again a compartmentalised lunchbox with some crudités and some cream cheese or hummus will make life easier for your child, keeping portions small and food accessible.

Vegetable choices that support parental pressures:

- Get your child to chop a carrot across its width. Show them how the cross-section of the carrot looks like an eye. Explain how carrots are full of beta-carotene which converts to Vitamin A in the body. Vitamin A is known as retinol and of course we have a retina in our eye. This is no coincidence. It is also no coincidence that we were told to eat carrots as children so that we could see in the dark. Vitamin A deficiency is one of the causes of night blindness. So having carrots in a lunchbox as a crudités for a dip or in a carrot cake, flapjack or muffin will be very well accepted because your child will have 'super powers'. For an older child it means they will be able to stay up later reading their book, when everyone else is in bed.

- A similar idea comes from walnuts that look surprisingly like a little brain. Scientists claim that walnuts help in developing over three dozen neuron-transmitters within the brain, enhancing the signalling and encouraging new messaging links between the brain cells. Walnuts, these mini-brains, are rich in the 'good fat' omega 3, so it will come as no surprise that if the brain was drained of water it would be 2/3 fat. Walnuts in a trail mix with some dried fruit or added to a date and walnut muffin will go down really well with the children who want to show how brainy they really are.

- Put kidney beans, which funnily enough heal and help maintain kidney function and are kidney shaped, into a salad or whizz them into a dip. This is a very visual connection and another cool fact for your child to share with their friends. There are many little helpers that nature gives us.

Fruit choices that support parental pressures:

- Talk to your children about the value of certain foods for our health. A tomato, for example, has four chambers and is red in colour. This is very similar to a heart which has four chambers and is also red in colour. Research has confirmed that tomatoes are loaded with lycopene, which is a chemical that really does improve and maintain the health of the heart and blood. So get your children thinking of tomatoes as heart food.

- Our lungs are made of branches of ever-smaller airways that finish up with tiny branches called alveoli. The alveoli look very similar to grapes. These grape-like protrusions allow oxygen to pass from the lungs to the blood stream. A diet containing lots of fresh grapes has been shown to reduce the risk of lung cancer and emphysema. Grape seeds also contain a plant chemical, which has been linked to a reduction in the severity of asthma.

- Bananas served in their very own banana sleeping-bag are something most children like, because they feel tucked-up and cared for. Imagine looking at a banana that has been bashed about in a school rucksack for the best part of the school day. It would be brown, bruised and squashed. Unappealing right? A fresh, unbruised banana will put a smile on your childs face. Not only do they taste great and provide a relase of much needed energy, they also contain a protein called tryptophan, which when digested converts into a neurotransmitter called serotonin, one of our mood-enhancing hormones. I like to think of the curve in the banana as the curve of a smile.

With both vegetables and fruit, why not set your children the challenge of creating their very own vegetable or fruit superhero, using their favourite vegetable or fruit as their raw material.

This chapter has provided you with the knowledge and tools to manage and overcome the pressure on parents to do the right thing by our children as far as the contents of their lunchbox are concerned. If you would like to put this knowledge and ideas into practice by using them to form your child's weekly menu plan then you can use the template provided in Appendix 1.

Chapter 6: Improvement Four – The Cheats Guide To Filling A Lunchbox With Healthy Foods

At the end of the day we are all busy people. The job of being a parent is an incredibly busy one and it never ceases to amaze me where the time goes to each day. I often say that if I could grow anything on trees, it wouldn't be money it would be time.

While researching this book, I spoke to a number of parents in order to understand the problems they face and to see how my knowledge may be able to help them. One of the biggest issues when producing packed lunches would seem to be a lack of time.

I have spoken to parents who will make a week's worth of sandwiches on a Sunday then freeze them and then take them out of the freezer on the morning that they need them. The sandwich is then fully defrosted by the time the child eats it.

I have spoken to parents who buy only pre-packaged items i.e. packaged yogurts, individually wrapped cheeses or string cheese, packets of crisps, cereal or chocolate bars and individual pieces of fruit.

And I have met parents who freshly prepare every single item of their child's lunchbox everyday.

While I do not want to get into the argument of which method is the worst or best, what I do see is the majority of parents use a combination of the above methods. I call this the middle ground. And it is this middle ground that I will use as the basis for this chapter. I am no different from any other parent, in that I have very little time. The only difference is that I obviously give more thought to packed lunchboxes than most, but then when you are a nutrition expert writing a book on the subject it is hard not to.

Based on the need to find quicker, easier ways of doing things and based on the fact that parents want/need to buy some 'quick fixes', I have put together two comprehensive lists. One outlines how to 'cheat' at making lunchboxes. This means ways in which you can speed up the process, and gives you short cuts without compromising the quality, taste or content of the lunchbox. The other list highlights some of the food products that you will find in most supermarkets and that can be put into the lunchbox either as they are or with just a little intervention. We all need some of these 'quick fixes' in our arsenal.

By the end of this chapter you should be able to put together a lunchbox in next to no time, using methods that speed up the preparation process, and with shop bought products.

Ways to save time or how to cheat at making up a lunchbox.

1. Make in bulk.

The best way to save time when producing food for children, is to bulk make foods and then freeze portions of them for use when you need them. This concept works brilliantly for baked goods. If you do find you have enough time one weekend or evening to bake some homemade lunchbox goodies, make more and freeze the rest. This way there is no waste, no duplicated effort and your child gets something homemade rather than shop bought.

2. Invest in a good food processor.

You will not believe how much time this will save you. Chopping up vegetables to pulverise into a soup later, or chopping them finely so they disappear into the texture of a muffin takes time. Here are some examples of how to put your food processor to good use:

- Whizz up veggies for vegetable flapjacks, muffins, vegetable fritters (see recipes in Chapter 9).

- Use the processor to finely chop the vegetables for a soup.

- Make dips such as hummus, smoked mackerel pate and guacamole in a minute.

- Whizz up fruits into a homemade smoothie or a fruit puree to be served with natural yogurt.

- Create pesto's with basil, sun-dried tomato and rocket. Use different nuts/seeds (pine nuts, cashews when allowed or sunflower seeds) and some cheese.

- Use the kneading function of your processor, which will help you make bread dough that you can use to make individual rolls.

3. Create a meal plan.

I am a real fan of meal planning. This simply means sitting down and thinking about what you are going to put into your child's lunchbox ahead of time. This planning process allows you to see what components of the COMPLETE and BALANCED lunchbox are missing and what needs to be added, or switched for something healthier. There's a whole chapter dedicated to this subject in Chapter 3 of this book. If planning is not your thing or you are stuck for ideas then visit **www.lunchboxdoctor.com** for weekly lunchbox menu plans.

4. Shop online.

Online supermarkets or supermarkets with an online presence have made it so easy to shop now, by also recommending products to you based on your previous purchases and saving lists (you could, for example, have three or four weekly menu plans which you rotate). It's a very simple process of ordering from your home or work computer and having the food delivered to your home. It is quick and easy. The other great upside to this is that you will not be persuaded by nagging children to buy junk food.

5. Have emergency standbys.

Have items in your food cupboard and freezer that you can use in emergencies. How many of us have been caught out before? Perhaps it is the day after you get back from your annual holiday or a weekend away. Perhaps you were just busy over the weekend, enjoying some family time and now Monday morning has come around and you think you have nothing suitable for a lunchbox. Well, let's think this through for a moment.

In the store cupboard:

- Do you have baked beans and tins of tuna or sardines? These are all useful if you have no fresh meat, fish or eggs in the house. Baked beans and sardines can be served as is. Tuna could be mixed with some tinned sweet corn and a little natural yogurt or mayonnaise.

- Packets of microwavable rice are really useful. Simply add some frozen vegetables and whisk up a couple of eggs for a very quick and tasty egg-fried rice. Add some low sodium soya sauce. Once cooled, refrigerate until your child is ready to go to school the next day then pop in an insulated lunchbox with a cold pack.

- Some companies produce some very hearty vegetable and bean or pulse soups like black bean and vegetable or lentil and vegetable. Be aware of the salt content, as some of these can be far too salty for younger, smaller bodies. However a good tinned soup, heated up and placed into a Thermos with some defrosted and toasted pitta wedges could be a hearty and filling lunch.

- Some cereals make a great snack. Granolas and oat-based cereals can be eaten from a container. Even flaked cereals are welcomed by many children just as they are. Watch for the sugar content. I tend to look for cereals with an absolute upper limit of 15g sugar per 100g of product but ideally you would use cereals with less sugar than this.

In the freezer:

- Frozen vegetables are an essential; slices of bread or pitta pockets are also incredibly useful for a quick sandwich or even as a pizza base.

- Filo pastry can easily be defrosted and used as a simple pie crust or container for an easy filling such as spinach and ricotta or some tinned ratatouille and grated cheese.

- Frozen berries and frozen sliced banana can be added to a smoothie made with long life milk, a non-dairy milk alternative and some ground nuts (if school allows) or seeds.

Store cupboard/ freezer list for standbys:

Tins	Tuna, sardines, hearty soups (with pulses), sweet corn, ratatouille
Food Cupboard	Microwave rice, seeds, nuts
Fridge	Natural yogurt, mayonnaise, cheddar cheese or Parmesan
Freezer	Frozen berries, frozen sliced banana, filo pastry, frozen vegetables
Long-life milk	Dairy (organic), non-dairy (rice, oat, almond, quinoa) milk

Figure 6.1:
Useful standby's.

Ways to cheat by buying lunchbox items straight from the shop or products that need very little preparation.

As someone who likes the quick and easy route, people often ask me what shop-bought products I consider acceptable for their children's lunchboxes.

It is so easy to get it wrong. Think about those plastic looking and plastic tasting cheese strings and squares, or the dippers with some processed cheese and salty, fatty crackers to dip in. All very easy to pick up at the supermarket and often on offer to make that decision even easier for you, but not balanced nutritionally.

Using the lunchbox checklist outlined in Chapter 2 of this book I will outline my preferred 'quick fix' choices by checklist item.

Carbohydrate quick fixes:

- Ready-made couscous salad with roasted vegetables
- Ready-made three-bean salad
- Packets of oatcakes
- Packets of oat biscuits
- Crisps – buy pre-packed rice crackers, baked crisps, root vegetable crisps, plain (corn) tortillas
- Lower sugar, no added colours or preservatives cereal bars
- Wholemeal baps, pittas, high fibre fruit loaf

Protein Quick Fixes:

- Cooked chicken breast
- Lean ham and turkey slices
- Smoked salmon
- Ready made sushi
- Small pots of reduced sugar and salt baked beans
- Edamame beans – ready to eat

Calcium Quick Fixes:

- Single natural yogurts
- Individually wrapped organic cheddar cheese
- 30g packs seeds and dried fruit
- Mini pots hummus

Vegetable Quick Fixes:

- Small tub olives
- Cans or cartons vegetables juice
- Sugar snaps

- Mini sweetcorn
- Pre-cut carrot sticks

Fruit Quick Fixes:

- Packs cubed fresh coconut
- Packs pomegranate seeds
- Small bags (30g) dried fruit
- Frozen berries
- Cherry tomatoes
- Berries or grapes, simply washed and put into a small serving container
- Apples, pears, bananas
- Fruit smoothies – individual portions
- Pre-sliced melon, mango or pineapple

Drinks – Quick Fixes:

- Small bottle water
- Rice milks cartons
- Milk cartons
- 100% fruit juice cartons
- Coconut water cartons or bottles

This chapter has provided you with the lots of quick fix ideas for your child's lunchbox. You will find a template in Appendix 1, which allows you to put these ideas into your child's weekly menu plan.

Chapter 7: Improvement Five – The Budget Lunchbox

We are all under financial constraints these days. The price of food has risen, as has the price of fuel. Sadly a lot of food is being transported, unnecessarily for commercial reasons. Frequently an apple grown in Kent will be transported to the West Country to be sold there, passing an apple grown in the West Country, heading for, you guessed it, Kent.

A job-for-life once existed, but now often parents will find themselves out of work for short periods of time and this does put further financial pressure on families. Food is a regular outgoing and needs to be put under the spotlight.

Supermarkets do sell some extremely reasonably priced food but obviously it is not all good quality. More often than not the cheapest items of food are the cheapest to produce, due to poor quality ingredients. Often supermarkets will try to entice us into buying certain goods by offering 'buy one get one free', (delightfully known as BOGOF) or reduced prices, which aren't really reduced. A friend told me how she stormed out of a well-known supermarket one day. She had picked up some beautiful cherries, which stated 'Half Price' and had a label underneath saying £4.99. She assumed that the £4.99 was to be halved at the checkout, so picked up the cherries believing that she was to pay £2.50. The cashier told her that the cherries were already half price, which meant that the cherries would have been £9.99 full price. Understandably she was very annoyed and simply couldn't believe anyone would have paid full price for them. It makes you wonder how long they were the full price for, if at all, before this amazing reduction.

There are lots of ways in which we can use the supermarket system to our own advantage. Of course I am grateful for the quantity and choice of foods available to us these days but we all know that the supermarkets are the big winners. If we shop smart and savvy then we can get what we want while helping them to provide us with the best foods. It's just a case of knowing how. The first point of this chapter is to understand how to play the supermarkets to your advantage, and reduce your weekly budget on lunchbox foods. The second section of the chapter covers my practical suggestions on how to put the budget lunchbox proposals into action to produce some of the most cost-effective, yet still complete and balanced, lunchboxes.

Navigate the supermarket.

- Go at the right time of day or the right day of the week. Sunday before 4pm closing time (so ideally sometime around 3pm) can reap great rewards.

- Look above and below eye-level - supermarkets are cleverly designed to entice you to buy more, with expensive items at eye level and the cheaper varieties on the lower levels. Take this into consideration when you are shopping. Look above and below eye level to find the best offer.

- Look at the 'price per 100g or per product' value to make comparisons between products.

- Go to the reduced section - pick up anything fresh that can be frozen such as fish, meat and any fruit or vegetables that you could use in baking to make banana loaf or carrot cake, vegetable muffins or scones for example. Supermarkets sell food at reduced prices if it has reached the *Sell By* date. The food is still fine to eat until it reaches its *Use By* date so this is a good way to save a few pounds. If it's not on your meal planner for this week either make a quick adjustment or pop it in the freezer and use it next week.

- Allow time - allow plenty of time to do your weekly shop so you can think about which are the cheapest options or hunt down any bargains.

- Leave the children at home - if it's at all possible. This gives you time to make informed decisions without any interference or nagging. If that's out of the question, see if you can find a creative way of involving them in your shopping - maybe counting out tomatoes or working out which cheese is the cheapest.

- Budget or Economy brands - try buying budget or economy own-brand foods, especially carbohydrates such as pasta and rice, and tinned goods such as tomatoes and fruit. They are often cheaper because they use less expensive packaging than the premium brands. Watch out for economy processed foods though as they often contain more sugar and salt than other brands.

Use local shops.

This depends on where you live of course. My sister lives in Whitstable, Kent and they have three greengrocers, two bakers, three butchers and four fishmongers in the town. There's plenty of competition to keep prices down. Being 'the garden of England' the produce is as local as possible.

Compare this to where my family lives in Buckinghamshire and we simply don't have any of these more traditional and privately owned shops on the High Street. This lack of availability and competition means you either go out of town, costing you money in fuel, or you accept what the supermarkets have to offer.

If you are lucky enough to have them locally then use your greengrocer, market, fishmonger and butcher. It's cheaper - you're not paying for all the packaging that ends up in the bin - so you'll be amazed at the amount you get for your money. What's more, once you're a regular and build up a rapport with the shopkeeper, it's highly likely that they'll throw in a freebie or two just for being a good customer.

Buy in bulk.

Buying in a larger size then dividing food up into individual portions will save you an astonishing amount of money. This works wonderfully well with cheese for example. Ditch the cheese spread and slices, as they tend to be of a lower quality than a good block of cheese. You can slice, dice and grate this to suit whichever way of preparation or presentation you have planned. Finding a good Italian delicatessen in your neighbourhood will help with saving money on Parmesan too. Buying a big portion (a whole or a half) of Parmesan can be used as and when you want and is a great way to save money. These cheeses last for a long time and you are not wasting money on packaging and labelling.

Avoid food wastage.

If you've made a bit too much food, don't throw it away. Evening meal surplus makes great packed lunches the following day, especially cooked carbohydrates like new potatoes, rice and pasta which can become great components of a salad for lunch, or soup which can be reheated and taken to school in a flask.

Leftover Sunday roast is a great way to save on processed sliced meats. Simply slice the meat off the joint or bone and use as is, chopped into a salad or in a sandwich or wrap.

Most foods will keep for up to two days in the fridge (not fish or seafood though) and can be used again. Always cool left over cooked food as quickly as possible. You can do this by placing in a cool part of the house or put the food in cold water. Then cover and store in the fridge or freezer until needed. Remember not to refreeze food that has already been frozen.

Use reusable pots.

Save money by ditching the cling film. Buy some containers with lids which can be reused, or just do as my parents' generation did, and we quite often do in our household - put a plate over the top.

Eat more vegetable protein.

Beans, lentils and pulses are all excellent forms of protein and significantly cheaper than meat and fish. They are also seriously tasty...vegetarians are onto a winner.

Budget lunchbox content ideas.

Now you know how to make your money go further let's look at some actual lunchbox ideas.

Carbohydrate budget choices:

- Leftover risotto – mould into balls. Pop a mini mozzarella ball into the centre. Coat in egg then breadcrumbs, rice crumbs or polenta and bake until hot all the way through (to reheat rice thoroughly and melt the mozzarella ball). Leave to cool before placing in your child's lunchbox with a cooler pack.

- Buy and freeze sliced wholemeal bread, wholemeal bagels and pitta breads.

- Make pizzas from flatbreads and then roll them up into a wrap.

- Use up old bread by making it into breadcrumbs to put on chicken, turkey, fish dipped in egg. These make cheap but healthy nuggets that could be served cold with some sort of dipping sauce (even a low sugar and salt ketchup).

- Use up old bread by gently sautéing into croutons for soups.

- Make your own bread (see recipes in Chapter 9).

Protein budget choices:

- Use pulses (beans, chick peas and lentils) in dips, soups and as an addition to salad.

- Roast a meat joint on a Sunday then slice the meat off rather than buy processed meats.

- Check out the 'cuts' area in the deli counter for cheap, oddly shaped bits of meats that are much lower in price.

- Use tinned fish, as it is an excellent source of protein and calcium.

- Use up eggs by making them into an omelette that can be eaten cold. A Spanish omelette (of sorts) can be achieved by putting cold sliced potatoes and vegetables (perhaps those left from the previous evening's supper) into the beaten egg mixture before cooking.

- Try roasting sunflower and pumpkin seeds, an easy task that children will enjoy doing. You can add a little soya sauce for even more flavour just prior to roasting.

Calcium budget choices:

- Buy cheese in bulk – be it a large chunk of cheddar or a big parmesan – then divvying it up into small portions: slice, grate or chop it into chunks to serve in the most appropriate fashion for your child and their preferences.

- Buy large pots of natural yogurt and divide into small portions, adding a topping i.e. a puree, honey, trail mix or granola.

- Low cost hummus is usually no less nutritious. Generally it contains less tahini (sesame seed paste) and more chickpeas. Tahini is the expensive ingredient. Equally making your own hummus can cost very little. Pulses, especially in some of the larger supermarkets or Asian supermarkets can cost less than the cost of a second-class stamp.

Vegetable budget choices:

- Buy organic vegetables only when you are going to eat the skin. The majority of unfavourable pesticides and herbicides in non-organic vegetables are contained within the skin. This is important to remember because you could save a lot of money by not buying organic unnecessarily.

- Buy UK and in season – parsnips for example can be bought in season for less than a pint of milk. Parsnip soup could be made for less than the price of a chocolate bar. I know which I would rather feed my children.

- Large jars of olives – decanted into smaller portions

Fruit budget choices:

- Buy organic varieties only when your child is going to eat the skin. So if it's a banana, pineapple, mango or melon don't bother going organic. If it is an apple, pear or grapes do think about choosing organic.

- Gathering fruit – be opportunistic – damsons, blackberries and apples can be easily made into purees and elderflowers can be made into cordial very easily.

- Pick Your Own – pick berries and freeze in bulk in the summer. Add these to baked goods such as muffins and flapjacks, to smoothies or just straight into natural yogurt. That way the berries and the natural coolness of the yogurt can act as your icepack, gently defrosting and ready to eat by lunchtime.

- Use tinned fruit in natural fruit juice either alone or mixed into natural yogurt.

Drink budget choices:

- If you can invest in a reasonably good water bottle, this will suffice.

- Cartons of drink tend to be cheaper if they contain more sugar and less fruit. Try to avoid 'fruit drinks' and opt for drinks that are still juice even if it is from concentrate. Concentrate simply means that the water from the juice is removed at source for cheaper transportation. However fresh juice in season is still the best possible juice from a nutritional standpoint.

This chapter has provided you with the knowledge and tools to select the lower cost and yet nutritionally sound options for your child's lunchbox. If you would like to put this knowledge and these ideas into practice by using them to form your child's weekly menu plan then you can use the template provided in Appendix 1.

Chapter 8: Food Allergy And Food Intolerance

Food allergy and food intolerance are often confused although generally not by those who suffer from them. They are caused by different bodily reactions and produce different symptoms.

Food Allergy:

Food allergies are the body's abnormal responses to foods. Such reactions are caused by the immune system's response to some food proteins.

The food that triggers an allergic reaction in the body is called an allergen. An allergen tends to trigger increasingly severe reactions in people the more they are exposed to it. When they eat the allergen, the body produces chemicals including histamine. This results in changes to the person's respiratory tract, digestive tract, skin and cardiovascular system. Ironically the reactions are your body's way of protecting itself from the allergen.

Allergic reactions can occur in minutes or up to two hours after the person has eaten the food. Symptoms include swelling of the tongue, diarrhoea and hives (raised, itchy rash). In severe cases, the allergic reaction can be fatal. In severe cases the reaction is anaphylaxis, which can be life threatening or even fatal.

Most common food allergens:

- Dairy foods including - milk, ice cream, yogurt, butter, and some margarines. However non-dairy foods that contain casein (milk protein) must be avoided. Prepared foods that contain milk protein ranges from breads to cold meats such as ham.

- Eggs. People are generally allergic to either the yolk or the white, more commonly the white, but due to the risk of cross-contamination the whole egg should be avoided. Remember eggs are also used in mayonnaise, baked goods, breads, pasta and batter on fried foods.

- Peanuts. Although these are a legume i.e. not a true nut but more like a pulse such as chickpeas and lentils, they are far more likely to be an allergen than other legumes. Foods that should be avoided include peanut butter, peanut oil, satay dishes and some desserts and chocolate.

- Tree nuts. This group of nuts include almonds, cashews (not technically a nut but grouped for identifying allergen purposes), pecans, walnuts, Brazil nuts, chestnuts, hazelnuts, macadamia nuts, pine nuts, and pistachios.

- Shellfish. This includes lobster, crab, prawns, clams, oysters, scallops and mussels. An allergy to one type of shellfish may indicate an allergy to others.

- Soy. This is another legume. Soy is an ingredient in many processed foods including crackers and baked goods, sauces and soups.

Parents tend to find out about food allergies when they introduce their baby to a certain food for the first or second time. If you are a parent with an allergenic child I am sure you are aware of the foods to be avoided and the places to avoid them, i.e. which products contain or are made alongside the allergen. There are some good resources for parents of allergenic children but the best by a long way, in my opinion, is called 'Food Allergy and Your Child' by Alice Willits and Deborah Carter (July 19, 2007). These are two parents who have children with food allergies and they have written an excellent book as a practical guide for parents.

Food intolerance:

Food intolerance is different from food allergy. Although rarely life threatening, it can cause severe discomfort. Reactions to a food can range from digestive discomfort and headaches to skin conditions. The way in which people react to a food to which they are intolerant varies. Some people have no digestive problems at all and suffer more from breathing difficulties or eczema. Others suffer mostly from digestive problems such as bloating, stomach cramps, wind and diarrhoea.

Some common food intolerances include:

1. Lactose intolerance is caused by a lack of the enzyme (called 'lactase') needed to break down lactose, the sugar in milk. A person with lactase deficiency can experience stomach pain and bloating for several hours after drinking milk.

2. Coeliac disease is caused by an autoimmune reaction to the protein in wheat, rye and barley. Coeliac disease can manifest itself, if left untreated, as anaemia due to poor iron absorption and osteoporosis due to poor

calcium absorption. These conditions result from the damage done to the gut by the gluten in wheat, rye and barley.

3. Reactions to chemical preservatives and additives, such as sulphites, monosodium glutamate, caffeine, aspartame and tartrazine. People can react to all normal foods too though these vary massively and depend on the individual. Dairy and wheat products tend to be the most common.

Fussiness can sometimes indicate food intolerance.

Children with either food allergy or food intolerance tend to steer clear of these foods naturally. However in the case of food intolerance there is also a phenomenon where the sufferer experiences an opioid like effect (i.e. a positive feeling) when they consume the food to which they are intolerant, so that the sufferer craves that food and eats more of it, making them more and more ill.

If your child is being 'fussy' around certain foods and/or eating a lot of one particular food group, you may want to consider food intolerance. Food intolerance can lead to nausea, bloating and discomfort as well as headaches, poor concentration levels and skin conditions.

What to do if you suspect food intolerance.

If you suspect food intolerance keep a food diary and identify foods eaten frequently. Among children the common offenders are wheat (bread, pasta, biscuits) and cow's milk (cheese, milk, yogurt). If you discover that your child's food diary is dominated by one or a few food groups and this is associated with symptoms of cravings, bloating and variable bowel habits i.e. sometimes very soft stools and sometimes stools that are hard to pass, then it is advisable to speak to a nutrition professional.

 One thing that is important to consider if you are the parent of a child with food allergy or intolerance, is to ensure that they have a balance of the right kinds of nutrients in their diet, and of course in their lunchbox. When an entire food group is eliminated, it is easy to become deficient in certain nutrients.

Nutrients provided by common food allergens, which could therefore become deficient, include the following:

- Dairy: vitamin A, vitamin D, riboflavin, pantothenic acid, vitamin B12, calcium and phosphorus

- Egg: vitamin B12, riboflavin, pantothenic acid, biotin and selenium

- Soy: thiamin, riboflavin, pyridoxine, folate, calcium, phosphorus, magnesium, iron and zinc

- Wheat: thiamin, riboflavin, niacin, iron and folate (if fortified)

- Peanut: vitamin E, niacin, magnesium, manganese and chromium

Your nutrition professional should be able to help you identify what the potential nutrient shortfalls are and how to make up for them. Below is a list of the alternative ways to incorporate possibly deficient nutrients into your diet.

Food sources of these nutrients:

- Vitamin A: pumpkin seeds, fish, beans
- Vitamin D: oily fish especially mackerel or tinned salmon
- Riboflavin: whole grains, poultry
- Niacin: potatoes, red meat, fish
- Pantothenic acid: legumes, fresh vegetables, mushrooms, rye flour
- Biotin: poultry, whole grains, soybeans
- Vitamin E: green vegetables, avocadoes, seeds, rice, oats, soy beans, legumes
- Selenium: fish and shellfish, poultry fruit, vegetable – broccoli, cabbage, mushrooms, onion, garlic
- Calcium: molasses, canned fish, seeds, dark green vegetables, parsley, cabbage, root vegetables, lentils
- Magnesium: seeds, dark green veg, whole grains, lentils, meats, poultry, fish, seafood, peas, garlic, potato skin, apricots, raisins, dried figs, bananas
- Manganese: root vegetables, leafy vegetables, oats
- Iron: molasses, shellfish, lean red meat, fish (especially sardines) cocoa, green veg, whole grains, seeds (especially sesame), dried fruits
- Chromium: molasses, whole grains, honey, oysters, vegetables, potatoes, parsnips, thyme, chicken

However, the best way to cope with food allergies and in order to limit the possibility of nutrient deficiencies you should pick the healthiest alternative/s to the allergen and using this/these in place of the problem food. Here are some suggestions:

Dairy:

- With bread or toast use good quality dairy free spreads such as those you can buy at health food stores (I highly recommend Vitaquell), olive oil, nut oils (freeze both in ramekins and use like butter once frozen to spread on to bread), coconut yogurt made simply from coconut milk (the only brand available in the UK at the time of writing is COYO), nut butters or seed butters.

- As milk alternatives use Oatly cream alternative which is fantastic for cooking with, rice milk, quinoa milk, almond milk, coconut water, or coconut milk.

- For sauces you can make pesto without cheese (you can use sunflower seeds in place of pine nuts), add aubergine to pasta sauces to create a 'creamy' texture.

- As a chocolate alternative you will find that Plamil Foods do a useful range of dairy free and nut free chocolate products.

Eggs:

- You can buy egg free mayonnaise (one such product is produced by Plamil), but also question why you need it and is there not a healthier alternative e.g. a raw slaw made with vinaigrette or tuna and sweetcorn bound together with oil, salad dressing or natural/coconut yogurt.

Baking (each substitute replaces one egg):

- Commercial egg replacer (this is a powder sold in boxes at most health food stores)
- 3 tbsp. silken tofu blended with the liquid in the recipe
- 2 tbsp. cornstarch, potato starch or arrowroot mixed with 2 tbsp. water
- 1 heaped tbsp. soy flour + 2 tbsp. water
- 1/2 banana, mashed*
- 1 tbsp. flax seeds + 110ml (1/2 cup) water blended for 1 to 2 minutes or until the mixture is thick and has the consistency of beaten egg whites*

*Favoured from a health perspective.

Wheat:

- Oats, found in oatmeal, flour, oatcakes, all of which contain small amounts of gluten

- Spelt which also contains gluten.

- Rye in bread, flour and crispbread. (Read the label to make sure they are 100% rye). Rye contains gluten.

- Barley flour, which still contains some gluten.

- Corn used in flour, pasta, cornflakes, crispbread, polenta, bread, nachos, tortillas, popcorn.

- Millet available as flakes, flour, crispbreads, bread and pasta.

- Buckwheat, also called 'kasha', found as flour and pasta. Buckwheat is NOT related to wheat, and can be used where wheat flour is used, except in breadmaking.

- Rice in flour, pasta, flakes, cakes and bread.

- Quinoa (pronounced 'keen-wa') can be purchased as flour, flakes and pasta.

- Amaranth, tapioca (from the cassava plant) arrowroot, gram flour (from chickpeas and used in poppadoms) and lentil flour can all be used as thickening agents.

Nuts:

- Use seeds in place of nuts in baking – sunflower seeds are a great alternative to almonds.

- Pumpkin and sunflower seeds can be made into 'butters' using a little oil or water as an alternative to peanut butter.

Tomatoes:

- Use beetroot or carrot juice in sauces – e.g. pasta sauce, bolognaise.

If your child has an intolerance specifically to lactose - low-lactose and lactose-free dairy products are available, as are lactase drops that can be added to dairy products. Also consider keeping small amounts of hard, aged cheeses (such as cheddar) in your child's diet which are lower in lactose, and yogurts that contain active cultures because they are easier to digest and much less likely to cause lactose problems.

If your child has a problem with bread but not other types of wheat based products such as pasta – try introducing what I call 'real' bread i.e. bought from a bakery. This generally contains just flour, water and yeast (or what is known as a 'starter' which would be used to make breads like sourdough). Yeast free breads should also be considered such as soda bread and soda farls.

Spelt is also often more easily tolerated than wheat and makes a very similar textured and flavoured loaf to a traditional wheat flour loaf.

If gluten is the problem there are a range of alternatives from rice cakes, corn cakes and gluten free crisp breads to gluten free breads and cereals.

These are my suggestions for the allergen free packed lunchbox:

Carbohydrate choices without allergens or intolerant foods.

- Pizza wrap – flatbread or soft flour tortilla (can buy gluten free) with passata and a mixture of vegetables including pitted black olives, some sweet corn and whatever else your child will eat. Bake these like a normal pizza, then cool and wrap/roll.

- Pasta (use buckwheat pasta or a standard gluten free pasta made from corn and rice for a gluten free version) salad with vegetables and mixed with olive oil.

- Vegetable muffins made using rice, gram or an alternative gluten free flour.

- Buckwheat pancakes with toppings.

- Rice paper parcels with finely sliced vegetables, cold shredded chicken and some Tamari (wheat free) soy sauce.

Protein choices without allergens or intolerant foods.

- Tinned tuna mixed with finely chopped peppers and olive oil.

- Sliced turkey or chicken from a roast joint or breast.

- Baked beans (reduced sugar and salt).

- Tahini-free hummus (see recipes in Chapter 9).

Calcium choices without allergens or intolerant foods.

- Gluten free oat flapjacks made with molasses.

- Dairy free cream cheese (see recipes in Chapter 9) with crackers and sliced black olives.

- Banana chocolate mousse (see recipes in Chapter 9).

Vegetable choices without allergens or intolerant foods.

- Vegetable kebabs – roasted Mediterranean vegetables threaded onto cocktails.

- Tinned sweet corn.

- Tinned or jars of olives.

Fruit choices without allergens or intolerant foods.

- Fresh fruit is best then you know it hasn't been prepared in an environment where any cross-contamination is possible.

- Tinned fruit.

- Pick your own fruit that you freeze for use in smoothies, baking or with a suitable yogurt.

Drink choices without allergens or intolerant foods.

- Dairy free milk alternatives – rice milk, quinoa milk, oat milk (contains gluten), almond milk (contains nuts).

- 100% fruit juice cartons.

- Bottled water.

Chapter 9: Recipes For Your Child's Lunchbox

Savoury Muffin

Use these savoury muffin and flapjack recipes as a base and play with different fillings to encourage your child to try vegetables.

225g (8oz) wholemeal flour
1 tsp baking powder
1 tsp bicarbonate of soda
2 tsp unrefined sugar
1 large egg, beaten
60g (2oz) unsalted butter, melted
150ml (5floz) milk
125g (4½oz) vegetable mix, grated
60g (2oz) cheese

Variations of fillings:
Courgette and ricotta
Carrot and Cheddar with pumpkin seeds
Pumpkin and date (only use 30g of date)

- Mix all dry ingredients and vegetables with cheese.
- Separately mix egg, milk and butter.
- Add the two sets of ingredients together.
- Mixture should be a 'dropping' consistency.
- Place in muffin cases in an oven at 190ºC/375ºF/Gas 5 for 15-20 minutes.

Savoury Flapjack

200g (7oz) porridge oats
200g (7oz) grated carrot
200g (7oz) grated courgette
200g (7oz) pecorino/parmesan, grated
2 small onions finely chopped
2 eggs beaten (or an egg alternative – see Chapter 8)
1 tsp dried mixed herbs

- Preheat the oven to 190ºC/375ºF/Gas 5.
- Grease a baking tray (Swiss roll tin size).
- Mix all the ingredients in the large bowl and press into the tray.
- Bake 25-30 minutes, until set and lightly browned.

Tip: Try a different nationality version i.e. Mexican with Monterey Jack cheese and peppers, or Greek with olives and feta.

Sweet muffin

225g (8oz) plain wholemeal flour
1 tsp baking powder
1 tsp bicarbonate of soda
70g (2½oz) unrefined sugar
60g (2oz) unsalted butter, melted and cooled
150ml (5floz) milk
2 small eating apples, cored (or 125g any fruit)
60g (2oz) raisins
Pinch of cinnamon

- Preheat oven to 190ºC/375ºF/Gas 5.
- Put the apples into a food processor and chop to a grated consistency. Take grated apple out of the machine and set aside.
- Place plain flour, baking powder, bicarbonate of soda, sugar and into a bowl.
- In a separate bowl, lightly whisk egg, butter and milk.
- Add the egg mix to the original bowl along with the grated apple, raisins and cinnamon. Stir until you achieve a 'dropping' consistency.
- Dollop the mixture into muffin cases to ⅔ full. Bake 15-20 minutes, until risen and golden.

Sweet Flapjack

70g (2½oz) pumpkin seeds
60g (2oz) runny honey
1 tbsp molasses
120g (4oz) butter
170g (6oz) rolled oats
45g (1½oz) dried fruit

- Grind seeds in a coffee grinder until a powder. In a saucepan gently heat the butter, molasses and honey until a liquid.
- Add oats, seeds, dried fruit and mix thoroughly so all ingredients are coated.
- Grease a baking tray and pour all the mixture into the middle of the baking tray. Flatten roughly into a flat square shape.
- Place in a pre-heated oven at 180C/360F/Gas Mark 4 for 20-25 minutes.
- Keep checking on them. When they are cooked leave them to cool on the tray. If you remove

them from the tray while hot they will crumble. Cut when they are cooling but not cooled.

Pea Fritter

1 tbsp mint
2 eggs
2 heaped tbsp natural yogurt
60g (2oz) easy-cook polenta
150g (5½oz) peas (fresh or defrosted)
½ tbsp honey
2-3 tbsp olive oil

- Put mint into your food processor and chop. Scrape down the sides. You may need to repeat this few times to get the mint fully chopped.
- Add the peas and chop to mix thoroughly with mint.
- Add all other ingredients except the olive oil. Mix on a low speed until all ingredients have come together and are evenly distributed.
- Heat oil in a frying pan.
- Drop spoonful's of mixture into the oil and fry for about 5 minutes, turning once, until golden brown on both sides.

Sweetcorn Fritter

2 tbsp coriander
2 eggs
3 tbsp natural yogurt
60g (2oz) easy-cook polenta
1 large tin sweet corn
2-3 tbsp olive oil

- Put coriander into your food processor and chop. Scrape down the sides. You may need to repeat this few times to get the coriander fully chopped.
- Add the sweet corn and chop to mix thoroughly with coriander.
- Add all other ingredients except the olive oil. Mix on a low speed until all ingredients have come together and are evenly distributed.
- Heat oil in a frying pan.
- Drop spoonful's of mixture into the oil and fry for about 5 minutes, turning once, until golden brown on both sides.

Tip: You can also use the egg frying rings in various shapes and sizes for a more fun effect e.g. star shaped fritters.

Rocket Pesto

40g (1½oz) basil leaves
40g (1½oz) rocket
80g (3oz) pecorino cheese
30g (1oz) pine nuts
1 clove garlic, peeled
150g (5½oz) extra virgin olive oil
salt to taste

- Wash the basil carefully and dry well on paper towels, taking care not to bruise it. Put all the ingredients except the oil and salt in to your food processor.
- Whizz these ingredients to a paste.
- Scrape down the sides of the food processor with a spatula.

- Add the oil and salt and whizz until all
  ingredients mixed.

Cashew Butter

400g (14 oz) raw cashews
¾ tsp flaked or fine sea salt
50g (1¾oz) cold-pressed organic rapeseed oil (also
known as canola oil)

- Grind the raw cashews in your food processor
  until fine and starting to become like a paste.
- Scrape down the sides of the food processor
  with a spatula.
- Add oil a bit at a time and blend again, scraping
  down the sides of the food processor and
  repeating as necessary until it becomes a lovely
  smooth, soft nut butter.
- Taste and add more salt if desired.

Mackerel Pate

300g (10½oz) smoked mackerel fillets
200g (7oz) probiotic Greek yogurt
2 tbsp creamed horseradish
1 lemon
Freshly ground pepper

- Peel the skin off the mackerel fillets and put
  into a blender with 100g (3½oz) of the
  yogurt, the juice of the lemon, some black
  pepper and the horseradish.
- Blend the ingredients until smooth then add the
  last 100g (3½oz) of yogurt but stir this in
  slowly.

Baby Croc Guac

2 ripe avocadoes, peeled and stoned
5g (⅕oz) fresh coriander, leaves and stems
70g (2½oz) red onion, finely diced
10g (⅓oz) lime juice
1 plum tomato, peeled and deseeded
40g (1½oz) extra virgin olive oil
Salt and pepper to taste

- Pop all ingredients in a food processor and process to desired consistency.

The following two dips are **not suitable** for those with family allergy to sesame seeds.

Hummus

400g (14oz) can chickpeas
Garlic clove, minced
⅓ cup V8 vegetable juice, beetroot juice or carrot juice
Juice of 1 lemon
2 tbsp tahini
2 tbsp oil

- Pop all ingredients in a food processor and process to desired consistency.

Aubergine and Tahini Dip

1 medium/large aubergine
1 clove garlic, crushed
70g (2½oz) tahini
100g (3½oz) olive oil
50ml (1¾floz) water
Juice 1 large lemon

- Grill aubergine slices, brushed with 25g olive oil.
- Put the cooked aubergine and all other ingredients in the food processor and process to creamy consistency.

Dairy Free Cream Cheese[3]

180g (6⅓oz) blanched almonds
180g (6⅓oz) sunflower seeds
150g (5⅓oz) lemon juice
3 cloves garlic
Freshly ground black pepper
¾ tsp sea salt
100ml-300ml (3½floz–10floz) water

- Soak the nuts and seeds overnight in water. Drain the next day when ready to use. Get rid of soaking water. You will need fresh water for the next stage.
- Place all the ingredients into a food processor with 100g (3½oz) of water. Process on full, pushing the ingredients down onto the processing blade with a spatula or wooden spoon.
- After 2-3 minutes the ingredients should be mixed to a 'cream cheese' consistency.

---

[3] Recipe adapted from an original recipe by Jo Whitton of Quirky Cooking

Banana Chocolate Mousse (dairy free)

3 bananas
340g (12oz) silken tofu
230g (8oz) 70% cocoa solids chocolate, melted over a
Bain Marie i.e. a bowl of chocolate placed in a saucepan
of boiling water (make sure the chocolate doesn't
touch the boiling water)

- Put all ingredients into a food processor and
  whizz to a mousse or cream pudding
  consistency.

Simple Bread Recipe

500g (17½oz) strong wholemeal or spelt bread flour
1½ tsp salt
1 tsp golden caster sugar
15g (½oz) butter (softened) or oil
1 sachet easy bake yeast
300ml (10floz) warm water
1 egg, beaten
Rolled oats or poppy seeds for the top

- In a large bowl mix the flour, salt, sugar and
  yeast. Add the butter or oil using your fingertips
  until blended in. Then add enough of the warm
  water to create a soft dough.
- Knead the dough on a lightly floured surface
  until it is smooth and elastic.
- Separate into 10 balls (you could, if you are
  creative, make the dough into similar sized
  shapes at this point for added fun and
  interaction with the children).
- Place the rolls on a baking tray and cover. Leave
  in a warm place like the airing cupboard until

they have doubled in size. This may take up to an hour.
- Preheat the oven to 230ºC/450ºF/Gas Mark 8. Brush the surface of the rolls with beaten egg and sprinkle on your chosen topping.
- Bake for 15 minutes then reduce the oven temperature to 200ºC/390ºF/Gas Mark 6 for the final 10 minutes until the rolls are golden brown and sound hollow when tapped underneath.
- Cool on a wire rack.

Raspberry and Tahini Flapjack

450g (16oz) porridge oats
250g (8.8oz) butter or dairy free spread
200g (7oz) unrefined sugar
1 heaped tbsp tahini
1 handful frozen berries

- Place the butter or dairy free spread, chopped into lumps, in a pan and pour over the sugar
- Heat slowly without stirring on a low heat until bubbles appear in the centre of the pan. Continue heating for another minute then stir in tahini and remove from heat. This is your toffee mixture.
- Pour the toffee mixture over the oats and mix well. Stir in the berries.
- Press into an oiled baking tray and bake at 200ºC/390ºF/Gas Mark 6 for 15-20 minutes until the top is golden brown.
- Cool, then cut up.

Chapter 10: What Have We Learnt?

Producing healthy, complete and balanced lunchboxes for your children doesn't have to be a chore. There is more choice than you thought before reading this book. For most parents it is the tedium of doing exactly the same task every day that drives them mad. As this book has shown, this doesn't have to be a tedious task. It can be a process which can be made quicker by planning, made easier by choosing shop bought produce, made cheaper by preparing and presenting food for much less money, but most importantly made more reassuring knowing that a nutrition expert has already done a lot of the thinking for you.

There's so much for parents to think about these days. From the expense of lunchboxes and the safety of the food within them, to the contents of the lunchbox and whether they are healthy enough, or whether they are nut and allergen free. The whole purpose of the previous nine chapters has been to make the task of identifying the best, most suitable and tasty lunchbox fillings, quicker and easier.

If you haven't had time to read every chapter in this book in detail, then let me give you an overview of the key learning points. That way you will be able to identify which sections are most suitable for you.

These are the key points:

There's a whole lot more that can go into a lunchbox than a sandwich. Children need variety and the same two pieces of bread with the same processed meat or cheese filling is going to get boring. It is boring for you to make every day and it is even more boring for them to eat it everyday. Most importantly it will start detracting from your child's health.

Lunchtime is an opportunity. It is a time in your child's life when they can form some great habits and start expressing an interest in healthy choices and variety. They will become experts at what foods are better for their health and which are not so good.

By following a simple formula, (a checklist) of all the food groups that should be considered for a healthy, balanced and complete lunchbox, you can be assured that the decisions you are making for your children, and hopefully the decisions they are also making and influencing, will be the right ones. They should have a say in what they prefer but allow them to express this preference once they have seen the full range of items on offer. At the moment your child's choices may seem limited to food items they already have in their lunchboxes, or those they see advertised on the TV, or even those food items placed at eye level in eye-catching colours in the supermarket. However once you have had the chance to try some of the foods, recipes and menu plans suggested, your child may start to exert their power of choice in ways you didn't think possible. Remember that I too like to go about things the quick and easy way. So be assured that not one of these methods, ideas, recipes or menu plans is going to be particularly arduous or time-consuming.

The checklist of food groups, as outlined in **Chapter 2** of this book, is as follows. You need to choose just one item from each group and voila, you have a complete and balanced lunchbox. How easy is that?

- Carbohydrates
- Proteins
- Calcium
- Vegetables
- Fruits
- Drink

Remember a little bit of time spent planning in advance can save a lot of time and hassle. Don't try to plan when you have the least time i.e. first thing in the morning when you are also trying to get yourself washed, dressed and fed as well as your children. Making breakfast multiple times AND making packed lunchboxes multiple times is no fun if you haven't got a plan. It is even more stressful if you haven't actually got the right foods in the house. In **Chapter 3** of this book I not only outline the importance of planning but HOW to plan. This single act has saved me money, time and arguments. It is really worth setting aside just 15 minutes in your week to carry out this task.

We are nowhere near meeting the 'five-a-day' vegetables and fruit portions promoted by the UK Government for consumption but this book is full to the brim of great and innovative ideas for including vegetables and fruit portions in your child's lunchbox so that this task will become second nature in next to no time. Remember eating five portions of fruit a day and no vegetables is not ideal if you want to give your child the full nutrient quota. Your child requires vegetables in their diet too. If your child is a reluctant eater when it comes to eating vegetables or any foods, then **Chapter 4** contains a whole host of ideas and information on how to encourage your child to eat a wider variety of foods from their lunchbox.

If the pressure we put on ourselves as parents to do the right thing is not enough, then the pressure from other parents, our children, our children's friends, the media and the Government all add to it. We can either choose to ignore these pressures and rise above them (this tactic is easier for adults than children though remember) or we can embrace these pressures and turn them to our advantage. In **Chapter 5** you can identify strategies for dealing with the pressures on parents including peer pressure.

Very few parents have the time required to trawl through supermarket shelves, read labels and work out the costs of food per kilogram. In **Chapter 6** of this book I have managed this feat and shown that there are some easy to obtain shop-bought foods that you will be really happy going into your child's lunchbox. They are not filled with added colours, preservatives and flavourings or unnecessary levels of salt and sugar. Although the contents of a lunchbox is my speciality subject, don't for a moment assume that I use home made produce entirely. If there is a cheat's way to do it I will find it. This is what **Chapter 6** is all about. After reading this chapter you'll be able to identify where it's ok to cheat and where it is not.

We have less money (relative to food costs) than we did even a year ago. This means that we need to know how to be supermarket and shop savvy. Knowing how to navigate the supermarket and knowing what to buy where is the trick to giving your child the best lunchbox at the least cost to you. **Chapter 7** provides you with a number of ways in which your child's lunchbox can be nutritionally sound while not costing you the earth.

Food allergies and intolerances are on the rise and the implications of this are both direct and indirect. For many parents they are experiencing food allergies in their families for the first time and realising that some of the more traditional aspects associated with school life, such as school lunches, cake sales and parties are fraught with potential danger. For the parents with children with no allergies a nut ban in school or recommendations on what not to include in lunchboxes, means less choice. However, in **Chapter 8** of this book there is an abundance of choice available to individuals who want to avoid allergenic and intolerant foods for their own purposes or because of policies in schools.

So you can see that although there is a lot of pressure on parents and although we might think our choices are limited, in fact there are loads of different options. There is even a very simple formula to follow to ensure that our children are getting a complete and balanced lunchbox every day. Obviously these 'rules' (I use that term lightly) can apply to other meals too. The options for meals eaten in the home are even wider. However picnics and lunches outside of the home environment or restaurant are covered by this book.

If you are struggling for new recipes and you like to prepare foods for your children's lunchboxes or if you are parent of a child with food allergies or intolerance and like to control their lunchbox food by cooking it yourself then **Chapter 9** provides some simple recipes for lunchbox foods for you to follow.

One final point is that a packed lunch carries the added responsibility of keeping the food safe to eat. That means keeping hot foods hot and cold foods cold. One study[4] found that less than a third of parents included a cold pack when packing yogurt, cold meats, sandwiches and other foods that need refrigeration. Cold packs are essential in centrally heated schools. A lunchbox that is insulated will be one step further to ensuring the food is safe to eat for lunchtime.

I hope you have enjoyed reading this book. I hope you have an abundance of practical ideas that you can put into action over the next school year or term. If you like what you have seen here and would like to join a community of like-minded parents who also care about what foods they put into their children's lunchboxes then come to **www.lunchboxdoctor.com**. There are a whole host of other benefits for you there, such as more recipes and meal plans to encourage you and your child to make healthier lunchbox choices every time, every day.

Jenny Tschiesche BSc (Hons) DipION, FdSc, CNHC Registered Practitioner

---

4 www.i-dineout.com/pages2007/lunch.9.4.07.html

Appendix 1

Here is your very own example planning table.

CHILDS NAME:	CARBOHYDRATE	PROTEIN	CALCIUM	FRUIT	VEGETABLE	DRINK
WEEKLY MENU PLAN						
MONDAY						
Spinach and ricotta muffin*	✓	✓	✓		✓	
Natural yogurt with apple fruit puree			✓	✓		
Mango hedgehog				✓		
Bottle of water						✓
TUESDAY						
Baby croc guac* with carrot stick, and sugar snap dippers					✓	
Left-over cooked rice with peas and sweet corn	✓				✓	
Apple				✓		
Two squares dark chocolate	✓					
Carton of milk		✓	✓			✓
WEDNESDAY						
Oatcakes and mackerel pate	✓	✓	✓			
Cucumber batons					✓	
Strawberries				✓		
Small pot granola	✓			✓		
Fruit juice with sparkling mineral water				✓		✓
THURSDAY						
Aubergine and tahini dip * and beetroot hummus with baked pitta chips	✓	✓	✓		✓	
Pear and fromage frais			✓	✓		
Two oat biscuits	✓					
Bottle of water						✓
FRIDAY						
Savoury flapjack* made with courgettes and carrots	✓	✓			✓	
Fruit salad				✓		
Natural yogurt and honey			✓			
100% fruit juice carton				✓		✓

* Recipes and instructions for all starred lunchbox content ideas can be found in Chapter 9

Planning Template

With this template you can plan one week's lunchbox contents for your child using the same checklist as shown previously.

CHILDS NAME:	CARBOHYDRATE	PROTEIN	CALCIUM	FRUIT	VEGETABLE	DRINK

WEEKLY MENU PLAN

MONDAY

TUESDAY

WEDNESDAY

THURSDAY

FRIDAY

Glossary

Anaphylaxis: Hypersensitivity to a substance, such as foreign protein or a drug that is caused by exposure to the substance.

Antioxidant: A substance that helps combat the negative effects on the body of poor dietary choices such as foods too high in sugar and fat.

Beta-Carotene: A vitamin found in certain colourful foods. Beta-carotene is converted to a form of vitamin A in the body.

Flavonoids: Water-soluble plant pigments that are beneficial to health.

Folate: A type of B vitamin that occurs naturally in dark green leafy vegetables, and members of the legume family, which include beans and peanuts.

Free Radical: A substance that, in excess, can cause cell damage in our bodies.

Legume: A seed, pod or other edible part of a leguminous vegetable. Examples include peanuts, peas and beans.

Lycopene: A red pigment in tomatoes which acts as an antioxidant.

Phytonutrient: A chemical compound that occurs naturally in plants. An example is beta-carotene.

3993139R00066

Printed in Germany
by Amazon Distribution
GmbH, Leipzig